A Simple S Grammar

With Exercises

R. J. Taylor

Head of Languages
Brockenhurst College

and

C. E. Alberry

Formerly Head of Spanish,
Priestlands School, Lymington

Hodder & Stoughton
LONDON SYDNEY AUCKLAND

British Library Cataloguing in Publication Data

Taylor, R. J.
  A Simple Spanish grammar with exercises
  I. Spanish language — Grammar
  I. Title   II. Alberry, C. E.
  468.2'421   PC4112

  ISBN 0 7131 0548 8

First published 1981
Ninth impression 1992

Printed in Great Britain for the educational publishing division of
Hodder and Stoughton Ltd, Mill Road, Dunton Green, Sevenoaks,
Kent by Athenaeum Press Ltd, Newcastle upon Tyne.

Preface

This book is intended to be used by average pupils and pupils of moderate ability, whose knowledge of English grammar is too limited to enable them to use, with ease, any of the more detailed Spanish grammars already available.

It is intended as a handy reference book for homework and exam revision, and as a companion to the major basic courses.

The contents aim to explain in simple terms the grammar points needed for first-level examinations.

Grammarians will no doubt notice omissions and superficial explanations at points where it seemed that elaboration would cause confusion. The aim is to give a simple grammar which will help pupils to understand the basic structure of Spanish.

R.J.T.
C.E.A.

Acknowledgement

Following the success of *A Simple French Grammar* by Susan Girelli, this book adopts a similar approach and presentation for teaching Spanish. We wish to express our appreciation to Susan Girelli for the inspiration her book provided.

Abbreviations

e.g.	for example	*N.B.*	note carefully
etc.	and so on	*pol. plur.*	polite plural
fam. plur.	familiar plural	*pol. sing.*	polite singular
fam. sing.	familiar singular	*plur.*	plural
fem.	feminine	*sing.*	singular
masc.	masculine		

Contents

Explanation of English terms used

Adjective

An adjective is a word that describes, or tells you something about, a person, place, animal or thing. **Big**, **pretty**, **tall**, **young** and all the colours are adjectives.

Adverb

An adverb tells you something about a verb, or action word. It can tell you *how* a thing is done, e.g. **quickly**, **well**, **happily**. It can tell you *when* an action is done, e.g. **often**, **always**, **usually**.

Apostrophe

This is a comma 'in the air' which shows you that a letter is missing. **He's** should really be **he is**, and the apostrophe shows that the **i** is missing.

Consonant

Consonants are all the letters of the alphabet, except the letters **A, E, I, O, U.**

Infinitive

This is the part of the verb that does not mention any person, but has **to** in front of it. **To make, to swim, to fall** are all infinitives.

Noun

A noun is a person, place, animal or thing, e.g., **John, a girl, the beach, the dog**.

Negative

A negative often shows that something is *not* to be done. **Not, never, no more** are all negatives.

Object

The object of a verb is the noun or pronoun that the verb acts on, and that is mentioned after the verb, e.g.:

We sold the car. **Car** is the object.
I saw them. **Them** is the object.

There can be a *direct object* and an *indirect object*. The above examples are direct objects. An indirect object usually has the word **to** before the noun or pronoun. To find out which is the indirect object, try to put *to* before the nouns/pronouns that come after the verb. The one that makes the most sense is the indirect object, and the remaining one (if any) is the direct object, e.g. I gave **him the present**. If you changed the order slightly you could put *to* in front of **him** (I gave the present to **him**), but it would not make sense if you put *to* in front of **the present**. So the indirect object is **him** and the direct object is **the present**.

The passive

The passive shows what *was done* to someone, rather than the action someone *did*, e.g.:

He was wounded. **Was wounded** is a passive verb.
They have been invited. **Have been invited** is a passive verb.

Past participle

The past participle of a verb is the part that usually goes with *has* and *have*. It shows that the action has taken place in the past. It often ends in **ed** but there are many exceptions.

You have walked. **Walked** is the past participle.
He has thrown. **Thrown** is the past participle.

Plural

This means that there is more than one noun mentioned. There is usually an **s** at the end of the noun, e.g. some cats, the ladies.

Possessive adjective

A possessive adjective shows who a person, place, animal, or thing belongs to, e.g. **his** son, **your** horse, **my** book.

Possessive pronoun

A possessive pronoun shows who a person, place, animal, or thing belongs to, but this time the person, place, etc., does not follow the possessive word, or is not mentioned at all, e.g.:

That dress is **hers**. This is **mine**.

Preposition

A word, often indicating position, which comes before a noun or pronoun, e.g. **at** the station, **to** the city, **with** my friend, **against** the wall.

Pronoun

A pronoun takes the place of a noun. Instead of repeating the name **John** all the time, you could use **he**. If you use a pronoun before a verb (as a subject), use the forms:

I, you, he, she, it, we, they.

If you put a pronoun after a verb (as an object), use the forms:

me, you, him, her, it, us, them.

For example, **Michael** likes **animals**.
  He likes **them**.

Reflexive verbs

These verbs do not exist in English in the same way as they do in Spanish. Reflexive verbs show that someone is doing something *to himself,* e.g.:

He shot **himself**. I scratched **myself**.

In English the verbs have a meaning without **himself, myself** etc. With Spanish reflexive verbs, the Spanish word for **myself, yourself**, etc. must always be there, even though it may have no separate meaning in English. (*See Chapters 21 and 22*)

Relative pronouns

Relative pronouns are the words **who, whom, which**, and **that**, which link sentences, e.g.:

She is the girl **who** bought my bike.
I found the pen **that** I had lost.

Often in English, **that** is used instead of all the other forms, or no word may be used at all, e.g.:

There's the book I want.
There's the book **that** I want.

Singular

Only one noun is mentioned, e.g., **a pig**, **the spade**, **a boy**.

Subject

The subject of a verb (or sentence) is the noun or pronoun which comes before the verb, and which does the action, e.g.:

John works hard. **John** is the subject.
She is knitting. **She** is the subject.

Tense

Tense indicates the different times when actions take place, e.g., present, future, past. Tense describes the time of the verb, and verbs have different forms for each tense, e.g.:

Present   I have
Future   I shall have
Past   I had

Explanations of individual tenses are given in the text.

Verb

A verb is a doing or being word which describes an action or a state: I **like**, he **works**, she **is**.

Vowel

Vowels are the letters **A, E, I, O, U**. The letter **Y** can sometimes be used as a vowel.

A Simple Spanish Grammar

1) Un, una = a, an

Every *noun* in Spanish is either *masculine* or *feminine*, even things like books and chairs. To show masculine words you use **un** = **a**, e.g.

un lápiz = a pencil, **un** libro = a book.

To show feminine words you use **una**, e.g.

una silla = a chair, **una** mesa = a table.

Exercise

Put **un** or **una** in front of these words:

a) casa b) bolígrafo c) perro d) goma e) muchacha

Note that most nouns ending in **o** are *masculine*, and most nouns ending in **a** are *feminine*.

2) El, la, los, las = the

There are four ways to say *the* in Spanish.

El: for masculine singular words, e.g.

el gato = the cat, **el** niño = the child.

La: for feminine singular words, e.g.

la vaca = the cow, **la** mujer = the woman.

Los: for masculine plural words, e.g.

los cuadernos = the exercise books, **los** chicos = the boys.

Las: for feminine plural words, e.g.

las cosas = the things, **las** niñas = the girls.

Exercise

Put **el**, **la**, **los**, **las** in front of these words:

a) tinta b) ventana c) mujeres d) globo e) manzana f) hotel g) pelota
h) papeles

3) Cardinal numbers 1 to 1000

1	**uno, una**	31	**treinta y uno**
2	**dos**	32	**treinta y dos**
3	**tres**	40	**cuarenta**
4	**cuatro**	41	**cuarenta y uno**
5	**cinco**	42	**cuarenta y dos**
6	**seis**	50	**cincuenta**
7	**siete**	51	**cincuenta y uno**
8	**ocho**	52	**cincuenta y dos**
9	**nueve**	60	**sesenta**
10	**diez**	61	**sesenta y uno**
11	**once**	62	**sesenta y dos**
12	**doce**	70	**setenta**
13	**trece**	71	**setenta y uno**
14	**catorce**	72	**setenta y dos**
15	**quince**	80	**ochenta**
16	**dieciséis**	81	**ochenta y uno**
17	**diecisiete**	82	**ochenta y dos**
18	**dieciocho**	90	**noventa**
19	**diecinueve**	91	**noventa y uno**
20	**veinte**	92	**noventa y dos**
21	**veintiuno**	100	**cien**
22	**veintidós**	101	**ciento uno**
23	**veintitrés**	102	**ciento dos**
24	**veinticuatro**	200	**doscientos/as**
25	**veinticinco**	300	**trescientos/as**
26	**veintiséis**	400	**cuatrocientos/as**
27	**veintisiete**	500	**quinientos/as**
28	**veintiocho**	600	**seiscientos/as**
29	**veintinueve**	700	**setecientos/as**
30	**treinta**	800	**ochocientos/as**
		900	**novecientos/as**
		1000	**mil**

The numbers not found here can be easily formed, e.g. **35** = **treinta y cinco**, **48** = **cuarenta y ocho**, and so on.

Special points

a) **Uno** loses its final **o** when in front of a masculine singular noun, e.g.

one egg = **un** huevo
but
How many eggs? **One**. = ¿Cuántos huevos? **Uno**.

The same rule applies to other numbers ending in *one*, e.g.

twenty-one years = **veintiún** años.

b) Remember the hundreds agree with the noun which they are describing, e.g.

seven hundred pesetas = **setecientas** pesetas

c) Other numbers do not alter, e.g.

four girls = **cuatro** chicas.

d) Remember: Between tens and units, where the number does not have *and* in English, it has **y** in Spanish, e.g.

seventy-six = **setenta y seis**.

Between hundreds and tens/units, where the number has *and* in English, it does not have **y** in Spanish, e.g.

one hundred and fifty = **ciento cincuenta**.

Special uses of numbers will be found under separate sections (e.g. **6) Dates**).

Exercise

Write out these numbers as Spanish words:

a) twenty-three b) thirty-five c) seventy-eight d) one hundred and fifty-two e) five hundred and eighty-nine

4) Ordinal numbers – first, second, third, etc.

first	**primero**		sixth	**sexto**
second	**segundo**		seventh	**séptimo**
third	**tercero**		eighth	**octavo**
fourth	**cuarto**		ninth	**noveno**
fifth	**quinto**		tenth	**décimo**

Special points

a) **Primero** and **tercero** lose their final **o** when placed before masculine singular nouns (see Chapter 29).

b) All ordinal numbers are adjectives, and behave as such (see Chapter 28).

c) The ordinal numbers beyond 10 exist, but are hardly ever used. Use cardinal numbers instead, e.g.

the **nineteenth** century = el siglo **diecinueve**.

d) With kings and queens the word *the* is not translated, e.g.

Isabel **segunda** = Elizabeth **II**, Luis **catorce** = Louis **XIV**.

Exercise

Write in Spanish:

a) the first day b) the fifth lesson c) Alfonso XIII d) the twentieth century

5) Days of the week, months of the year

Days

Monday	**lunes**		Friday	**viernes**
Tuesday	**martes**		Saturday	**sábado**
Wednesday	**miércoles**		Sunday	**domingo**
Thursday	**jueves**			

Months

January	**enero**		March	**marzo**
February	**febrero**		April	**abril**

May	**mayo**	September	**septiembre**
June	**junio**	October	**octubre**
July	**julio**	November	**noviembre**
August	**agosto**	December	**diciembre**

Note that capital letters are not used with the days and months in Spanish.

Special points

a) Use **el** in front of the day to translate *on Monday*, etc., e.g.
I shall arrive **on Monday** morning. = Llegaré **el lunes** por la mañana.

b) **Los** in front of the day gives the idea of *every*, e.g.

los jueves = **on Thursdays** = **every Thursday**

All the days have the same form in the plural, except **sábado** and **domingo**, which become **los sábados** and **los domingos**, e.g.

Voy al cine **los sábados**. = I go to the cinema **on Saturdays**.

c) **En** or **en el mes de** means *in* with months, e.g.

Vamos a ir a Madrid **en julio/en el mes de julio**. = We are going to Madrid **in July**.

Exercise

Put into Spanish the following:

a) on Monday b) on Sundays c) on Tuesday morning d) in December e) in May

6) Dates

The normal numbers 2–31 are used with dates and *of* is translated by **de** in front of the month and the year, e.g.

the **3rd of** May = **el tres de** mayo
the **20th of** August = **el veinte de** agosto
the **13th of** July, 1980 = **el trece de** julio de mil novecientos ochenta

For the first of the month use either **el primero** or **el (día) uno**, e.g.

the **first** of November = **el primero** de noviembre
                    el (día) uno de noviembre

No word for *on* is needed before a date, just use **el**, e.g.

On the 2nd of February = **el** dos de febrero

En is used with years to mean **in**, e.g.

in 1980 = **en** mil novecientos ochenta
in 1520 = **en** mil quinientos veinte

Exercise

Write the following out as Spanish words:

a) 4th March b) 19th October c) 1st April d) on 30th December e) in 1855

7) Time

To tell the time in Spanish you need to know the numbers 1–29, and remember to *put the hours before the minutes*.

Es **la una** = It is **one o'clock**
Son **las dos** = It is **two o'clock**
Son **las tres** = It is **three o'clock**
etc. until
Son **las doce** = It is **twelve o'clock**

Son **las cuatro y cinco** = It is **five past four**
Son **las cuatro y diez** = It is **ten past four**
Son **las cuatro y cuarto** = It is **a quarter past four**
Son **las cuatro y veinte** = It is **twenty past four**
Son **las cuatro y veinticinco** = It is **twenty-five past four**
Son **las cuatro y media** = It is **half past four**
Son **las cinco menos veinticinco** = It is **twenty-five to five**
etc.

Special points

Es **mediodía** = It is **midday**
Es **medianoche** = It is **midnight**

Notice that you should use **Es** for **It is** only before **la una**. Otherwise use **Son**.

The word for *at* is **a**, e.g.

Nos veremos **a** las diez y media. = We will meet **at** half past ten.
Salgo de casa **a** las ocho y media. = I leave home **at** half past eight.

Exercise

Put the following into Spanish:

a) It is two o'clock b) It is twenty to twelve c) It is twenty-five past three
d) It is half past one e) At a quarter past ten

8) Weather and seasons

el verano = the summer
el otoño = the autumn
el invierno = the winter
la primavera = the spring

en verano = in summer
en el verano = in the summer
etc.

Here are some common descriptions of the weather:

Hace bueno, hace buen tiempo. = It is fine.
Hace malo, hace mal tiempo. = The weather is bad.
Hace calor. = It is hot.
Hace frío. = It is cold.
Hace fresco, hace fresquito. = It is cool.
Hace sol. = It is sunny.
Hace viento. = It is windy.
Hace un tiempo borrascoso. = It is stormy.
(El cielo) está nublado. = The sky is cloudy, it is cloudy.
Hay niebla. = It is foggy.
Hay neblina. = It is misty.
Llover. = To rain.
Llueve. = It rains.
Está lloviendo. = It is raining.
Nevar. = To snow.
Nieva. = It snows.
Está nevando. = It is snowing.

Special points

To express *very* you must use **mucho/a** (much), to express *so* you must use **tanto/a** (so much), when using expressions with **hace** and **hay**, e.g.

Hace **mucho** calor. = It is **very** hot.
Hace **tanto** frío. = It is **so** cold.

To put the above expressions into the *past* use **hacía** for **hace**, and **había** for **hay**, e.g.

Hacía mal tiempo ayer. = The weather **was** bad yesterday.

In the same way **llueve** becomes **llovía**, and **está lloviendo** becomes **estaba lloviendo**, e.g.

Estaba lloviendo anoche. = **It was raining** last night.

Some useful expressions:
Un día caluroso = A hot day
Una noche fría = A cold night

Exercise

Write two sentences describing the weather of each of the four seasons e.g.

En el otoño hace viento.

9) Some, Any

Some or *any* is translated by **algún**, **alguna** in the singular, and either **unos**, **unas** or **algunos**, **algunas** in the plural.

Examples

¿Tienes **algún** papel? = Do you have **any** paper?
Tengo **alguna** carne. = I have **some** meat.
Aquí están **unos** (**algunos**) sellos. = Here are **some** stamps.
¡Deme **unas** (**algunas**) galletas! = Give me **some** biscuits.

Special points

Often the word for *some* or *any* is missed out.

Example

¿Has comprado vino? = Have you bought (any) wine?

In a negative sentence *any* is translated by **ningún, ninguna, ningunos** or **ningunas**. (See Chapter 20)

Exercise

Fill in the spaces with the appropriate word.

a) ¿Tiene Vd. . . . dinero?
b) He comprado . . . zapatos.
c) ¡Mándeme . . . revistas!
d) Necesito . . . harina.

10) Combinations of a and de

A (**to**) combines with **el** to give **al**
De (**of**) combines with **el** to give **del**.
There is no change in the other forms.

Examples

Doy un libro **al** profesor. = I give a book **to the** teacher.
Es la madre **del** chico. = She is the mother **of the** boy.
Vamos **a las** tiendas. = We are going **to the** shops.
Regresan **de la** panadería. = They come back **from the** baker's.

Exercise

Put **a, al, a la, a los**, or **a las** in front of the following:

a) chicas b) libros c) cine d) estación e) Pedro f) Sevilla

Put **de, del, de la, de los**, or **de las** in front of the following:

a) Granada b) hombres c) muchacho d) Fernando e) hermanas f) tía

11) De of possession

In English we can use *'s* or *s'* to show possession, e.g. *Susan's* pencil, *the girls'* mother, etc. In Spanish you *must* turn it back to front, and use **de** = **of**, e.g.

It's **Susan's pencil**. = Es **el lápiz de Susana**.
(It is *the pencil of Susan*.)
Mr. Gómez is **Susan's father** = El sr. Gómez es **el padre de Susana**.
(Mr. Gomez is *the father of Susan*.)

De *never* shortens to **d'**, even before a vowel.

Exercise

Fill in **de** or a combination of **de**. (See Chapter 10)

a) Es el coche . . . profesor.
b) Aquí están los libros . . . Miguel.
c) Pablo lleva la chaqueta . . . Pedro.
d) Estoy buscando la cartera . . . alumna.
e) Conozco a la madre . . . chicos.

12) Subject Pronouns – I, you, he, she, it, we, they

yo = I	**nosotros/as** = we
tú = you	**vosotros/as** = you
él = he	**ellos** = they (masculine)
ella = she	**ellas** = they (feminine)
Vd. = you	**Vds.** = you

The subject pronouns are normally omitted in Spanish, except for **Vd.** and **Vds.**, which are normally included. It is clear from the verb ending which subject pronoun is meant, e.g.

Habl**o** = **I** speak
Tom**amos** = **We** take.

The subject pronouns are used for emphasis, e.g.

Yo no quiero ir al cine, pero **ella** sí. = **I** do not want to go to the cinema, but **she** does.
¿Quién es? Soy **yo**. = Who is it? It's **me**.

The four forms of *you* should be carefully differentiated:

tú = you, when talking to one member of the family, a child or a friend.
Vd. = you, when talking to someone to whom you want to be polite or

show respect, e.g. pupil talking to the teacher, customer talking to shop assistant.

vosotros = you, when talking to more than one member of the family, friends or children.

Vds. = you, when talking to more than one person to whom you want to be polite or show respect.

In future chapters the *you* forms will be referred to in the following way:

tú = *fam. sing.* (i.e. *familiar singular*)
Vd. = *pol. sing.* (i.e. *polite singular*)
vosotros = *fam. plur.* (i.e. *familiar plural*)
Vds. = *pol. plur.* (i.e. *polite plural*)

It and *they*, when referring to things are rarely expressed in Spanish, e.g.

Llueve. = It rains.
Son rojos. = They are red.

13) Verbs

To be able to use a verb in Spanish you must know the *infinitive*, that is, the part of the verb which mentions no person but which usually has *to* in front of it in English, e.g. *to sing, to cry, to eat*, etc. The two most common examples where you must use the infinitive in Spanish where the word *to* does not appear in English are after *must* and *can*, e.g. he must come, I can swim.

Note: an infinitive is used after the following prepositions, where in English the verb ends in *-ing*: **antes de** (before), **después de** (after), **sin** (without), **al** . . . (on . . .). For example:

antes de entrar = before entering; **al llegar** = on arriving

When two verbs are together with the second verb in the infinitive, sometimes you need to put **a** or **de** before the infinitive. Here is a list of the most important ones:

ir a	to go	**acabar de**	to have just . . .
venir a	to come	**cesar de**	to stop
empezar a	to begin	**terminar de**	to stop
ponerse a	to begin	**dejar de**	to stop
invitar a	to invite	**tratar de**	to try
ayudar a	to help	**haber de**	to have to
enseñar a	to show, teach	**tener ganas de**	to want
volver a	to . . . again	**darse cuenta de**	to realise

In some cases there is *no* preposition. The most common are: **querer** (to want), **desear** (to want), **poder** (to be able), **deber** (to have to), **lograr** (to manage), **conseguir** (to manage), **decidir** (to decide), **preferir** (to prefer).

Examples

Voy a trabajar = I am going to work
Ha cesado de llover = It has stopped raining
No puede venir = He cannot come

A regular verb is one which follows a regular pattern in the various tenses, and most verbs are regular. Unfortunately some of the most commonly used verbs are irregular, and have to be learned individually.

There are three kinds of regular verb, and the infinitives have the endings: **ar**, **er**, **ir**, e.g.

cantar = to sing
correr = to run
subir = to go up

14) Two important irregular verbs – ser and estar = to be

a) *Present tense*

ser	estar	
soy	estoy	I am
eres	estás	you are (*fam. sing.*)
es	está	he, she, it is
Vd. es	Vd. está	you are (*pol. sing.*)
somos	estamos	we are
sois	estáis	you are (*fam. plur.*)
son	están	they are
Vds. son	Vds. están	you are (*pol. plur.*)

b) *Explanation of use*

One of the most important things to learn in basic Spanish grammar is the difference of usage between **ser** and **estar**. If you follow these simple rules you should not make mistakes.
Estar is used to express *position* e.g.

Madrid **está en** España = Madrid **is in** Spain
¿**Dónde estás?** **Estoy en** el jardín = **Where are** you? **I am in** the garden

Estar is used to describe a *temporary state or condition*, e.g.

Estoy muy cansado = **I am** very tired
¿**Estás** listo? = **Are you** ready?

Some of the most common adjectives which are used with **estar**:

contento = happy, **triste** = sad, **cansado** = tired, **ocupado** = busy, **enfermo** = ill, **malo** = ill, **bien** = well, **preocupado** = worried, **listo** = ready, **solo** = alone, **abierto** = open, **cerrado** = closed.

Ser is used to describe a *permanent state or condition*, as in the following cases:

a) name
   ¿Quién es Vd.? =   Who are you?
   Yo soy Pedro. =   I am Pedro.
b) nationality
   ¿Es Vd. italiano? = Are you Italian?
   No soy italiano, soy español. = I'm not Italian, I'm Spanish.
c) colours
   Los libros son rojos. = The books are red.
d) professions and jobs
   María es secretaria. = Maria is a secretary.
   Pedro es profesor. = Pedro is a teacher.
e) permanent conditions
   Juan es muy inteligente. = Juan is very intelligent.
   Eres alto y gordo. = You are tall and fat.
   (Implies you will *always* be tall and fat.)

Special points

Notice that **estar** cannot be immediately followed by a noun as its object, e.g.

   Es un hombre malo. = He is a bad man.

The adjectives *rich, poor, young* and *old* are considered to be permanent, and are used with **ser**, e.g.

   Eres todavía **joven**. = **You are** still **young**.

Exercise

Put the correct form of **ser** or **estar**.

a) Nosotros . . . jóvenes.
b) ¿Dónde . . . el hospital?
c) ¿Qué . . . esto?
d) ¿De dónde . . . tú?
e) Ellos . . . en el jardín.

f) Málaga . . . en España.
g) Yo . . . profesor de inglés.
h) ¿Por qué . . . Vd. triste?
i) ¿Qué hora . . . ?
j) ¿ . . . vosotros españoles?

15) Ar verbs

a) *Present simple tense*

The infinitive of all verbs in this group ends in **ar**. To form the present simple tense, find the *stem* of the verb by removing **ar** from the infinitive e.g.

cantar = to sing	*stem* – **cant**
hablar = to speak	*stem* – **habl**

Add the following endings to the stem:

yo – **o**	**nosotros** – **amos**
tú – **as**	**vosotros** – **áis**
él ⎫	**ellos** ⎫
ella ⎬ – **a**	**ellas** ⎬ – **an**
Vd. ⎭	**Vds.** ⎭

Here is an example of the present simple tense of a regular **ar** verb, **cantar** = to sing:

canto = I sing	**cantamos** = we sing
cantas = you sing (*fam. sing.*)	**cantáis** = you sing (*fam. plur.*)
canta = he, she, it sings	**cantan** = they sing
Vd. canta = you sing (*pol. sing.*)	**Vds. cantan** = you sing (*pol. plur.*)

Exercise

Fill in the correct form of the verb given in brackets.

a) (Yo) . . . un periódico. (comprar)
b) (Nosotros) . . . en una tienda. (trabajar)
c) Vds. . . . temprano. (llegar)
d) (Vosotros) . . . al profesor. (hablar)
e) Mi madre . . . la comida. (preparar)

b) *Present continuous tense*

To translate *I am drinking, he is listening*, etc. into Spanish we use the present continuous tense. This is formed by using the present tense of the verb **estar** (to be) (see Chapter 14), and the present participle of the verb. To form the present participle of an **ar** verb, remove the **ar** from the infinitive, and replace it with **ando**, e.g.

cantar – **cant** – **cantando**
hablar – **habl** – **hablando**

Present continuous tense of **hablar** = to speak, talk:

estoy hablando = I am speaking
estás hablando = you are speaking (*fam. sing.*)
está hablando = he, she, it is speaking
Vd. está hablando = you are speaking (*pol. sing.*)
estamos hablando = we are speaking
estáis hablando = you are speaking (*fam. plur.*)
están hablando = they are speaking
Vds. están hablando = you are speaking (*pol. plur.*)

Exercise

Fill in the correct form of the verb given in brackets.

a) Vds. . . . (bailar)
b) (Yo) . . . una carta a mi madre. (mandar)
c) (Nosotros) . . . al fútbol. (jugar)
d) La chica . . . una limonada. (tomar)
e) ¿Por qué . . . (tú)? (llorar)

16) Er verbs

a) *Present simple tense*

The infinitive of all verbs in this group ends in **er**. To form the present simple tense, find the stem of the verb by removing **er** from the infinitive e.g.

beber = to drink   stem – **beb**
comer = to eat   stem – **com**

Add the following endings to the stem:

yo – o	**nosotros – emos**
tú – es	**vosotros – éis**
él ⎫	**ellos** ⎫
ella ⎬ **– e**	**ellas** ⎬ **– en**
Vd. ⎭	**Vds.** ⎭

Here is an example of the present simple tense of a regular **er** verb, **beber** = to drink:

bebo = I drink   **bebemos** = we drink
bebes = you drink (*fam. sing.*)   **bebéis** = you drink (*fam. plur.*)
bebe = he, she, it drinks   **beben** = they drink
Vd. bebe = you drink (*pol. sing.*) **Vds. beben** = you drink (*pol. plur.*)

Exercise

Fill in the correct form of the verb given in brackets.

a) Vd. . . . manzanas. (vender)
b) (Vosotros) . . . en el instituto. (comer)
c) (Nosotros) . . . periódicos. (leer)
d) Juan . . . vino blanco. (beber)

b) *Present continuous tense*

As with **ar** verbs, the present continuous tense of **er** verbs is formed by using the present tense of **estar** (to be) (see Chapter 14), and the present participle of the verb. To form the present participle of an **er** verb, remove the **er** from the infinitive, and replace it with **iendo**, e.g.

vender – vend – vendiendo
comer – com – comiendo

Present continuous tense of **beber** = to drink:

estoy bebiendo = I am drinking
estás bebiendo = you are drinking (*fam. sing.*)
está bebiendo = he, she, it is drinking
Vd. está bebiendo = you are drinking (*pol. sing.*)
estamos bebiendo = we are drinking
estáis bebiendo = you are drinking (*fam. plur.*)
están bebiendo = they are drinking
Vds. están bebiendo = you are drinking (*pol. plur.*)

Exercise

Fill in the correct form of the verb given in brackets.

a) Los hombres . . . patatas en el mercado. (vender)
b) (Yo) . . . un café con leche. (beber)
c) La chica . . . (coser)
d) (Nosotros) . . . en la calle. (correr)
e) ¿Qué . . . (tú)? (comer)

17) Ir verbs

a) *Present simple tense*

The infinitive of all verbs in this group ends in **ir**. To form the present simple tense, find the stem of the verb by removing **ir** from the infinitive, e.g.

vivir = to live	stem – **viv**
escribir = to write	stem – **escrib**

Add the following endings to the stem:

yo – o	nosotros – imos
tú – es	vosotros – ís
él ⎫	ellos ⎫
ella ⎬ – e	ellas ⎬ – en
Vd. ⎭	Vds. ⎭

Here is an example of the present simple tense of a regular **ir** verb, **vivir** = to live:

vivo = I live	**vivimos** = we live
vives = you live (*fam. sing.*)	**vivís** = you live (*fam. plur.*)
vive = he, she, it lives	**viven** = they live
Vd. vive = you live (*pol. sing.*)	**Vds. viven** = you live (*pol. plur.*)

Exercise

Fill in the correct form of the verb given in brackets.

a) (Yo) . . . en Madrid. (vivir)
b) Vd. . . . regalos de sus amigos. (recibir)
c) Juan . . . postales a su hermana. (escribir)
d) Las muchachas . . . al autobús. (subir)
e) (Vosotros) . . . la ventana. (abrir)

b) *Present continuous tense*

As with **ar** and **er** verbs the present continuous tense of **ir** verbs is formed by using the present tense of **estar** (to be) (see Chapter 14), and the present participle of the verb. To form the present participle of an **ir** verb, remove the **ir** from the infinitive, and replace it with **iendo**, e.g.

escribir – escrib – escribiendo
recibir – recib – recibiendo

Present continuous tense of **escribir** = to write

estoy escribiendo = I am writing
estás escribiendo = you are writing (*fam. sing.*)
está escribiendo = he, she, it is writing
Vd. está escribiendo = you are writing (*pol. sing.*)
estamos escribiendo = we are writing

estáis escribiendo = you are writing (*fam. plur.*)
están escribiendo = they are writing
Vds. están escribiendo = you are writing (*pol. plur.*)

Exercise

Fill in the correct form of the verb given in brackets.

a) (Nosotros) . . . cartas a nuestros padres. (escribir)
b) (Tú) . . . la puerta. (abrir)
c) (Yo) . . . los huevos. (batir)
d) Los chicos . . . la calle. (subir)

18) Radical changing verbs in the present tense

Many verbs change their root or stem when it is stressed in the present tense. This change occurs in all parts except the 'nosotros' and 'vosotros' forms, because the stress falls on the ending in these two parts.

a) **e** changes to **ie** when stressed, as in **perder** = to lose:

pierdo	perdemos
pierdes	perdéis
pierde	pierden
Vd. pierde	Vds. pierden

b) **o** changes to **ue** when stressed, as in, **encontrar** = to find:

encuentro	encontramos
encuentras	encontráis
encuentra	encuentran
Vd. encuentra	Vds. encuentran

Other kinds of radical change are explained in Chapter 55.

Exercise

Change the infinitive into the correct form of the present tense:

a) Yo . . . manzanas. (querer)
b) ¿ . . . Vd. venir conmigo? (poder)
c) ¿Qué . . . tú de esto? (pensar)
d) Nosotros . . . siempre. (perder)

e) ¿ . . . Vds. español? (entender)
f) Me . . . el pie. (doler)
g) ¿Cuándo . . . vosotros? (volver)
h) Tú . . . muy bien, ¿verdad? (recordar)

19) Tener = to have

a) *Present tense*

tengo = I have
tienes = you have (*fam. sing.*)
tiene = he, she, it has
Vd. tiene = you have (*pol. sing.*)

tenemos = we have
tenéis = you have (*fam. plur.*)
tienen = they have
Vds. tienen = you have (*pol. plur.*)

b) Notice these special expressions which use **tener:**
tener . . . años = to be . . . years old
tener calor = to be hot (of a person)
tener frío = to be cold (of a person)
tener prisa = to be in a hurry
tener hambre = to be hungry
tener sed = to be thirsty
tener suerte = to be lucky
tener sueño = to be sleepy, tired
tener razón = to be right
tener miedo = to be afraid
tener que . . . = to have to . . .

In these expressions, if you wish to include the word for *very*, you must translate it by **mucho/a**, *not* **muy**, e.g.

Tengo **mucha** suerte. = I am **very** lucky.

Exercise

Fill in the correct part of **tener:**

a) Andrés . . . doce años.
b) (Nosotros) . . . suerte.
c) ¿ . . . Vds. miedo del toro?
d) Yo . . . una bicicleta nueva.
e) Los niños . . . sueño.

f) ¿ . . . (tú) un lápiz?
g) ¿No . . . Vd. frío?
h) ¿ . . . (vosotros) los libros?
i) María . . . que hacer sus deberes.

20) Negatives – not, never, no-one, no more, no longer, nothing, neither, neither . . . nor

The negative is very easy in Spanish. All you need to do to make a sentence negative is to put **no** before the verb, e.g.

Hablo francés = I speak French
_No hablo francés = I do **not** speak French
Está lloviendo = It is raining
No está lloviendo = It is **not** raining

Negative words:

nunca, jamás = never, not ever
nadie = nobody, not anyone
nada = nothing, not anything
ninguno (a, os, as) = no (*adjective*), none (*pronoun*), not any
tampoco = neither, not either
ni . . . ni = neither . . . nor, not any . . . or

Special points

When the negative words come after the verb you must place **no** before the verb.

Examples

No voy **nunca (jamás)** al cine. = I **never** go to the cinema.
No veo a **nadie** por aquí. = I **can't** see **anyone** around here.
No tengo **ningún** amigo. = I **don't** have **any** friends (a friend). (See Chapter 29)
No tengo **ni** hermanos **ni** hermanas. = I **haven't any** brothers **or** sisters.
No me gusta **tampoco.** = I **don't** like it **either.**

But when the negative word comes before the verb, **no** is not required.

Examples

Nunca salgo con él. = I **never** go out with him.

Nadie ha llamado hoy. = **Nobody** has called today.
Tampoco me gusta. = I **don't** like it **either**.

Notice the two ways of expressing *no more, no longer*:

No tengo más dinero. = I have **no more** money.
Ya no vienen. = They **don't** come **any** more. They **no longer** come.

Negative words can stand on their own.

Examples

¿Quién ha salido? **Nadie.** = Who has gone out? **Nobody.**
¿Qué quieres hacer? **Nada.** = What do you want to do? **Nothing.**
¿Has visitado España? **No, nunca.** = Have you visited Spain? **No, never.**

Sino

Sino means **but** when it contradicts a negative, e.g.

No voy a Francia **sino** a España. = I am not going to France **but** to Spain.
La película no es sólo mala **sino** también es aburrida. = The film is not only bad **but** it is also boring.

Exercise

Make the following sentences negative:

a) Siempre voy a cenar con amigos los sábados.
b) Veo algo debajo de la mesa.
c) Yo quiero ir al teatro también.
d) Tengo algo que decirte.
e) ¿Tiene Vd. algún dinero?
f) Alguien llama a la puerta.
g) Yo voy al cine. Yo también.

21) Reflexive pronouns

yo ──────→**me**		**nosotros** ──────→**nos**	
tú ──────→**te**		**vosotros** ──────→**os**	
él ──────→**se**		**ellos** ──────→**se**	
ella ──────→ **se**		**ellas** ──────→**se**	
Vd. ──────→**se**		**Vds.** ──────→**se**	

Reflexive pronouns are used with reflexive verbs (see Chapter 22). Reflexive verbs in Spanish would be incomplete without the above pronouns. They can also be used to give the idea of *myself, yourself,* etc. and *one another, each other.*

Examples of the different uses of the reflexive pronoun:

a) **Se** levanta. = He gets up.
   Me acuesto a las nueve. = I go to bed at nine o'clock.

b) **Se** mira en el espejo. = She looks at **herself** in the mirror.
   Nos vemos todos los jueves. = We see **each other** every Thursday.

The reflexive pronoun is usually placed immediately in front of the verb, but it is joined to the end of the verb when it is:

a) an infinitive (see Chapter 22)
b) a present participle (see Chapter 22)
c) a command which is not negative (see Chapter 23)

Special point

The pronoun **se** is also used as an *impersonal* pronoun to express the fact that something is generally done in a certain place. In English, this is expressed by the *passive* (see Chapter 54). For example:

En España **se** bebe mucho vino. = In Spain a lot of wine **is drunk**.
Se cultivan manzanas en Asturias. = Apples **are grown** in Asturias.
Se habla español en Argentina. = Spanish **is spoken** in Argentina.

22) Reflexive verbs

a) *Present simple tense*

Reflexive verbs can be found in any of the three groups of verbs (**ar, er, ir**) and follow the same pattern, except that you must remember to use the reflexive pronoun (see Chapter 21), because otherwise it would not make sense in Spanish. Here is an example, **levantarse** = to get up:

me levanto = I get up	**nos levantamos** = we get up

te levantas = you get up
        (*fam. sing.*)
	os levantáis = you get up
	        (*fam. plur.*)

se levanta = he, she, it gets up	**se levantan** = they get up

Vd. se levanta = you get up
        (*pol. sing.*)
	Vds. se levantan = you get up
	        (*pol. plur.*)

Special point

If the infinitive of the reflexive verb is used along with another verb which is the main verb of the sentence, you must remember to change the reflexive pronoun, so that it matches the subject of the main verb, e.g.

Vamos a **levantarnos.** = We are going to get up.

In the above example the temptation would be to put **se** instead of **nos** on the end of the infinitive. However, the reflexive pronoun must match the subject and in this case **nos** must be used.

Further examples

No me gusta **levantarme.** = I don't like getting up.
María va a **peinarse.** = Maria is going to comb her hair.

Exercise

Fill in the correct form of the verb given in brackets.

a) (Yo) . . . muy tarde. (levantarse)
b) Los niños . . . en el dormitorio. (peinarse)
c) (Vosotros) . . . temprano. (acostarse)
d) Pepe . . . todos los días. (bañarse)
e) Vamos a . . . en el jardín. (sentarse)

b) *Present continuous tense*

This is formed in the normal way by using the present tense of **estar** (to be) (see Chapter 14) and the present participle of the verb. You must remember to include the reflexive pronoun. It can be placed *either* in front of the part of **estar** you are using, *or* it can be tagged on to the end of the present participle. If it is placed at the end of the present participle, you must remember to put an accent on the present participle to keep the stress on the correct part of the word (see Chapter 58) e.g.

Me estoy lavando *or* Estoy lavándo**me.** = I am washing myself.
Nos estamos bañando *or* Estamos bañándo**nos.** = We are bathing.

Exercise

Fill in the correct part of the verb given in brackets. Give two answers for each sentence.

a) Pablo . . .. (peinarse)
b) Vd. . . .. (lavarse)
c) Las mujeres . . . los dientes. (limpiarse)
d) (Yo) . . . en el lago. (bañarse)
e) (Nosotros) . . .. (acostarse)

23) Commands

a) *Familiar – tú, vosotros*

If you want to give a command using **tú** or **vosotros**, you must form it as follows:

Ar verbs

Take the infinitive, and remove **ar**,
tú form – add **a**   **vosotros** form – add **ad**

Er verbs

Take the infinitive, and remove **er**,
tú form – add **e**   **vosotros** form – add **ed**

Ir verbs

Take the infinitive, and remove **ir**,
tú form – add **e**   **vosotros** form – add **id**

There are some irregular forms of the **tú** command, and these have to be carefully learned. Here is a list:

Decir = to say, tell	**di**
Hacer = to do, make	**haz**
Ir = to go	**ve**
Poner = to put	**pon**
Salir = to leave	**sal**
Ser = to be	**sé**
Tener = to have	**ten**
Venir = to come	**ven**

Here are some examples:

Di la verdad. = Tell the truth.
Haz tu trabajo. = Do your work.
Pon el libro en la mesa. = Put the book on the table.
Sé sensato. = Be sensible.

There are no irregular forms of the **vosotros** command.

If you want to express the **tú** or **vosotros** command in the negative, you have to form it in a different way. For the stem, take the **yo** form of the present tense and remove **o**. For the ending add the following:

	tú	**vosotros**
ar verbs	es	éis
er verbs	as	áls
ir verbs	as	áis

Examples

Habla despacio. = **Speak** slowly. (*singular*)
No hables tanto. = **Don't speak** so much. (*singular*)
Hablad más. = **Speak** more. (*plural*)
No habléis tan rápidamente. = **Don't talk** so quickly. (*plural*)

The four examples above are of a regular **ar** verb. The regular **er** and **ir** verbs follow the same pattern, but use their own endings as shown above.

The verbs which have an irregular form of the **tú** command form their negative in a regular way, e.g.

No tengas miedo. = **Don't be afraid.**
No vengas sin tu padre. = **Don't come** without your father.

For irregular forms of the negative **tú** and **vosotros** commands see the **tú** and **vosotros** forms of the present subjunctive in the irregular verbs table. (see Chapter 59)

Exercise

Make the following phrases into **tú** commands, using the verb in brackets:

a) . . . con mi padre. (hablar)
b) . . . tus deberes. (hacer)
c) No . . . hasta las diez. (salir)
d) . . . la puerta. (abrir)

Make the following phrases into **vosotros** commands, using the verb in brackets.

a) . . . vuestros libros. (buscar)
b) . . . a vuestro cuarto. (subir)
c) No . . . tanto. (beber)
d) . . . la pizarra. (mirar)
e) No . . . a casa todavía. (ir)

b) *Polite – Vd., Vds.*

If you want to give a command using **Vd.** or **Vds.**, you must take the **yo** form of the present tense, remove the **o**, and add the following endings:

	Vd.	**Vds.**
ar verbs	e	en
er, ir verbs	a	an

These forms, unlike the **tú** and **vosotros** forms, do *not* change for the negative.

Vd. and **Vds.** are often placed after the verb in the command. For radical changing verbs in commands see Chapter 55. For irregular forms of the **Vd.** and **Vds.** commands see the *he* and *they* forms of the present subjunctive in the irregular verbs table (Chapter 59).

Examples

Singular

Tome (Vd.) el libro. = **Take** the book.
No olvide (Vd.) de venir. = **Don't forget** to come.
Lea (Vd.) el artículo. = **Read** the article.
Suba (Vd.) en seguida. = **Go up** at once.

Plural

Bajen (Vds.) aquí. = **Get off** here.
No fumen (Vds.) por favor. = **Don't smoke** please.
No vengan (Vds.) todavía. = **Don't come** yet.

Exercise

Make the following phrases into **Vd.** commands using the verb in brackets:

a) . . . paciencia. (tener)
b) . . . con cuidado. (escuchar)
c) No . . . los anuncios. (mirar)
d) . . . de la casa. (salir)
e) No . . . sus cosas en la mesa. (poner)

Make the following phrases into **Vds.** commands using the verb in brackets:

a) . . . sus fotos. (traer)
b) . . . las noticias. (oír)
c) . . . detrás de nosotros. (subir)
d) No . . . el agua. (beber)
e) . . . sus nombres. (escribir)

c) *How to express 'Let's'*

There are two ways of expressing *Let's* in Spanish.

i) The more formal method is to take the **yo** form of the present tense, remove the **o** and add:

ar verbs   **emos**
er and **ir** verbs   **amos**

Examples

Bajemos. = **Let's go down.**
Salgamos. = **Let's leave.**
Subamos. = **Let's go up.**

ii) The more conversational method is to say **Vamos a** . . . with the infinitive, e.g.

Vamos a ver. = **Let's** see.
Vamos a tomar una copa. = **Let's** have a drink.

Note that **Vamos** on its own means **Let's go.**

Exercise

Express *Let's* by using both methods with the verb in brackets.

a) . . . los cuadernos. (mirar)
b) . . . la verdad. (decir)
c) . . . pronto. (salir)
d) . . . a los abuelos. (escribir)
e) . . . la prueba. (hacer)

d) *Commands with reflexive verbs*

Reflexive pronouns (see Chapter 21) are tacked on to the end of the command, but go before the verb when the command is made negative. Object pronouns behave in the same way, and these are explained in Chapter 40.

Examples of reflexive pronouns in commands:

Levántate. = Get up. (*fam. sing.*)
No te levantes. = Don't get up. (*fam. sing.*)
Levántese. = Get up. (*pol. sing.*)
No se levante. = Don't get up. (*pol. sing.*)
Levantémonos. = Let's get up. (note the **s** is omitted)
No nos levantemos. = Let's not get up.
Levantaos. = Get up, (*fam. plur.*) (note the **d** is omitted)

No os levantéis. = Don't get up. (*fam. plur.*)
Levántense. = Get up. (*pol. plur.*)
No se levanten. = Don't get up. (*pol. plur.*)

Note the accents. The explanation for this is in Chapter 58.

Exercise

Put the following verbs into the **tú** and **vosotros** commands:

lavarse, sentarse, acostarse, bañarse, despertarse.

Make the answers to the above exercise negative.

24) Personal a

When a person is the object of a verb in Spanish you must place **a** between the verb and the person.

Examples

He **visto a Juan** en la calle. = I have see Juan in the street.
Estoy buscando a mi primo. = I am looking for my cousin.
Esperan al Sr. Gómez. = They are waiting for Mr. Gomez.

Notice how to form questions:
¿A quién esperan? = Who are they waiting for?
¿A quiénes buscan? = Who are they looking for?

Special points

You do not usually put **a** after **tener**, e.g.

No tengo hermanos. = I haven't any brothers or sisters.

You do not put **a** when you are not specifying the person, e.g.

Busco una criada. = I am looking for a maid.
Detesta las mujeres. = He hates women.

Exercise

Put the personal **a** where necessary:

a) Busco un policía.
b) ¿Has visto mi hermano?

c) Tiene nueve hijos.
d) Nunca escucha la profesora.
e) Espero el Sr. Fernández.

25) Question forms

Any statement can be made into a question in Spanish by putting a question mark at the end of the sentence, and an inverted question mark (¿) at the beginning of the sentence, e.g.

¿Vas al cine? = Are you going to the cinema?

When making questions with **Vd.** or **Vds.**, it is common to put **Vd.** or **Vds.** after the verb.

Examples

¿**Va Vd.** a casa? = Are you going home?
¿**Quieren Vds.** acompañarnos? = Do you want to come with us?

Reference list of question words:

¿**Cuánto, a, os, as**? = How much/How many?
¿**Cómo**? = How?
¿**Dónde**? = Where?
¿**Por qué**? = Why?
¿**Cuándo**? = When?
¿**Qué**? = What?
¿**Cuál(es)**? = Which, what?
¿**Quién(es)**? = Who?

Note that **Qué** can also be used in an exclamation to translate **What (a)**, and **Cuánto** can be used to mean **What a lot**, e.g.

¡**Qué** día! = **What** a day!
¡**Qué** niños! = **What** children!
¡**Cuánto** dinero! = **What** a lot of money!

Exercise

Fill the space with the most appropriate question word.

a) ¿ . . . está a la puerta?
b) ¿ . . . van a llegar?

c) ¿ . . . hay en la mesa?
d) ¿ . . . está mi perro?
e) ¿ . . . no has cenado?

26) Prepositions with names of towns, countries and other places

Translate *in* in English into **en** in Spanish.
Translate *to* in English into **a** in Spanish.
When *at* means *in* translate into **en** not **a**.

Examples

I live **in** England. = Vivo **en** Inglaterra.
I am going **to** Spain. = Voy **a** España.
He is going **to** Madrid. = Va **a** Madrid.
The children are **at** school. = Los niños están **en** la escuela.
My parents are going home. = Mis padres van **a** casa.
My grandfather is **at** home. = Mi abuelo está **en** casa.

Special point

Notice you must always say **llegar a**, e.g.

We shall arrive **in/at** Paris at ten o'clock. = Llegaremos **a** París a las diez.

Exercise

Put in the correct word in Spanish.

a) Nuestros tíos viven . . . Málaga.
b) Los niños están . . . casa.
c) Mañana vamos . . . Madrid.
d) Me gustaría ir . . . Escocia.
e) Mi tía está . . . la iglesia.
f) Llegaremos . . . Londres en diez minutos.

Reference list of the names of some countries:

Africa = **África**
Australia = **Australia**
Austria = **Austria**
Belgium = **Bélgica**

Canada = **el Canadá**
England = **Inglaterra**
Europe = **Europa**
France = **Francia**

Germany = **Alemania**
Great Britain = **Gran Bretaña**
Holland = **Holanda**
Ireland = **Irlanda**
Italy = **Italia**
Russia = **Rusia**

Scotland = **Escocia**
Spain = **España**
Switzerland = **Suiza**
U.K. = **Reino Unido**
U.S.A. = **Estados Unidos**
Wales = **Gales**

27) Prepositions with means of transport

These expressions should be learned by heart:

by air = **en avión**
by bike = **en bicicleta/en bici**
by boat = **en barco**
by bus = **en autobús**
by car = **en coche**
by coach = **en autocar**
on foot = **a pie**

on horseback = **a caballo**
by lorry = **en camión**
by van = **en camioneta**
by moped = **en motocicleta**
by motorbike = **en moto**
by taxi = **en taxi**
by train = **en tren**

Exercise

Put in the correct preposition:

a) Vamos a Madrid . . . tren.
b) Viaja siempre . . . avión.
c) La familia va a dar un paseo . . . coche.
d) Los niños van al centro . . . pie.
e) Voy a volver . . . autobús.

28) Adjectives

Adjectives in Spanish must be masculine or feminine, singular or plural, to match the *noun* they are describing. You will probably learn adjectives in their masculine singular form, e.g. **bonito** = **pretty**, **viejo** = **old**. Note that most adjectives end in **o** in their masculine singular form. From the chart below you can see that you should change the final letter in order to make the adjectives match their nouns.

---

masculine singular – stays the same
feminine singular – replace **o** with **a**
masculine plural – replace **o** with **os**
feminine plural – replace **o** with **as**

Examples

masculine singular	*feminine singular*
el coche **viejo**	la casa **vieja**

masculine plural	*feminine plural*
los coches **viejos**	las casas **viejas**

If the adjective ends in any other letter in the masculine singular, there is usually no change in the feminine singular (see special point for exceptions), and both plural forms add **es** to the masculine singular form, or **s** if the masculine singular form already ends in **e**.

Examples

masculine singular	*feminine singular*
el sombrero **azul**	la falda **azul**
el capítulo **interesante**	la lección **interesante**

masculine plural	*feminine plural*
los sombreros **azules**	las faldas **azules**
los capítulos **interesantes**	las lecciones **interesantes**

Special point

Adjectives of nationality and those ending in **án**, **ón**, **or** (exceptions – **mejor**, **peor**, **mayor**, **menor**, **superior**) have a separate feminine form, e.g.

un libro **francés** = a French book
una chica **francesa** = a French girl
los coches **franceses** = the French cars
las mujeres **francesas** = the French women

Note that **inglés**, **francés** and **alemán** lose their accents in the feminine and plural forms. The reasons for this are explained in Chapter 58.

Position of adjectives

Usually the adjective comes after the noun it describes, e.g.

una chaqueta **barata** = a cheap jacket
unos zapatos **sucios** = some dirty shoes

Some adjectives can be placed before the noun, and here is a list of the most common ones:

mucho = a lot of, many
poco = a few
varios = several
otro = (an)other
cierto = certain

Note that **otro** and **cierto** must never have **un, una** in front of them.

The other adjectives which come before the noun and behave in a special way are mentioned in Chapter 29. The following adjectives change their meaning slightly when placed before the noun:

nuevo = new
pobre = poor

> *Examples*
>
> Tenemos un coche nuevo. = We have a new car. (i.e. brand new)
> Tenemos un nuevo coche. = We have a new car. (i.e. different)
> Es un hombre pobre. = He is a poor man. (i.e. he has no money)
> Es un pobre hombre. = He is a poor man. (i.e. wretched)

Exercise

Fill in the correct form of the adjective given in brackets.

a) Me gusta la corbata . . . (rojo)
b) Es una casa . . . (grande)
c) No me gustan los coches . . . (francés)
d) Los chicos son muy . . . (gordo)
e) He comprado una camisa . . . (azul)
f) Aquí están dos chicas . . . (bonito)
g) Mi hermana es . . . que mi hermano. (mayor)

29) Special adjectives

These adjectives drop the letter o when used in the masculine singular form and when the adjective comes before the noun.

bueno	– **buen**	**tercero**	– **tercer**
malo	– **mal**	**alguno**	– **algún**
primero	– **primer**	**ninguno**	– **ningún**

Note the accent on the last two examples. The reasons for this are explained in Chapter 58.

Note also that the adjective **grande** is shortened to **gran** when it is used in front of either masculine or feminine nouns. In this case it usually means *great* rather than *big*.

Examples

Es un **buen** libro. = It is a **good** book.
Es un **mal** alumno. = He is a **bad** pupil.
El **primer** día del mes. = The **first** day of the month.
Vamos a leer el **tercer** capítulo. = We are going to read the **third** chapter.
No tengo **ningún** papel. = I haven't got **any** paper.
¿Tienes **algún** dinero? = Do you have **any** money?
Es un **gran** amigo mío. = He is a **great** friend of mine.
Era una **gran** reina. = She was a **great** queen.

Exercise

Fill in the correct form of the adjective.

a) Es un . . . día. (malo)
b) Madrid es una . . . ciudad. (grande)
c) Hemos terminado el . . . capítulo. (primero)
d) Es un . . . perro. (bueno)
e) Hemos tomado nuestro . . . vaso de vino. (tercero)

30) Possessive adjectives – my, your, his, etc.

	singular		plural	
	masculine	*feminine*	*masculine*	*feminine*
my	**mi**	**mi**	**mis**	**mis**
your (*fam. sing*)	**tu**	**tu**	**tus**	**tus**
his	**su**	**su**	**sus**	**sus**
her	**su**	**su**	**sus**	**sus**
your (*pol sing.*)	**su**	**su**	**sus**	**sus**
our	**nuestro**	**nuestra**	**nuestros**	**nuestras**
your (*fam. plur.*)	**vuestro**	**vuestra**	**vuestros**	**vuestras**
their	**su**	**su**	**sus**	**sus**
your (*pol. plur.*)	**su**	**su**	**sus**	**sus**

Since these are adjectives they must match the word they describe, just like any other adjective (see Chapter 28). Be careful *not* to match the possessive adjective with the person who is the owner, e.g.

They see their mother. (**Their** in Spanish has to be matched with **mother.**) = Ven a **su madre.**

Examples

Aquí está **mi** padre. = Here is **my** father.
Aquí están **tus** libros. = Here are **your** books. (*fam. sing.*)
Estamos buscando a **nuestras** amigas. = We are looking for **our** friends.
Los chicos trabajan en **su** dormitorio. = The children work in **their** bedroom.

Special point

As **su** can have so many meanings, you can add **de él, de ella, de Vd.**, **de ellos, de ellas, de Vds.** to avoid confusion, e.g.

Es **su** libro **de ella.** = It is **her** book.
Es **su** casa **de Vds.** = It is **your** house. (*pol. plur.*)

It is also common to find:

Es **el** libro **de ella.**
Es **la** casa **de Vds.** etc.

Exercise

Fill in the correct form of the possessive adjective given in brackets.

a) Veo a . . . hermano cada día. (your – *fam. sing.*)
b) Aquí están . . . primas. (my)
c) Hemos perdido . . . libros. (our)
d) Han vendido . . . coche. (their)
e) ¿Dónde está . . . casa? (your – *pol. plur.*)

31) Possessive pronouns – mine, yours, his, etc.

Possessive pronouns are used instead of possessive adjectives and a noun. The same rules for matching apply (see Chapter 30).

	singular		*plural*	
	masculine	*feminine*	*masculine*	*feminine*
mine	el mío	la mía	los míos	las mías
yours (*fam. sing.*)	el tuyo	la tuya	los tuyos	las tuyas
his	el suyo	la suya	los suyos	las suyas
hers	el suyo	la suya	los suyos	las suyas
yours (*pol. sing.*)	el suyo	la suya	los suyos	las suyas
ours	el nuestro	la nuestra	los nuestros	las nuestras
yours (*fam. plur.*)	el vuestro	la vuestra	los vuestros	las vuestras
theirs	el suyo	la suya	los suyos	las suyas
yours (*pol. plur.*)	el suyo	la suya	los suyos	las suyas

Examples

Es **tu libro**. Es **el tuyo**. = It's **your book**. It's **yours**.
¿Es **el perro de María**? Sí, es **el suyo**. = Is it **Mary's dog**? Yes, it's **hers**.
¿Es **la chaqueta de Pedro**? Sí, es **la suya**. = Is it **Peter's jacket**? Yes, it's **his**.

Special points

a) **El suyo, la suya** etc. have six possible meanings: his, hers, yours (*pol. sing.*), theirs (*masc.*), theirs (*fem.*), yours (*pol. plur.*). To avoid confusion **suyo, suya** etc. may be replaced by **de él** (his), **de ella** (hers), **de Vd.** (yours – *pol. sing.*), **de ellos** (theirs – *masc.*), **de ellas** (theirs – *fem.*), **de Vds.** (yours – *pol. plur.*), e.g.

No me gusta **su casa**. Prefiero **la de Vd.** = I don't like **his house**. I prefer **yours**.

b) When the possessive pronoun comes immediately after a part of **ser**, it is very common to leave out **el, la, los** and **las**, e.g.

Esta casa es **suya**. *or* Esta casa es **de Vd.** = This house is **yours**.

Exercise

Fill in the correct form of the possessive pronoun given in brackets.

a) No me gusta su coche. Prefiero . . . (ours)
b) Aquí están unos cuadernos. Son . . . (theirs – *fem.*)
c) Aquí está un bolígrafo. Es . . . (yours – *fam. sing.*)
d) Aquí están unas manzanas. ¿Son . . . (his)? No, son . . . (hers)
e) ¿Dónde está tu regla? . . . está en la mesa. (mine)

32) This, these, that, those, as adjectives

Use the following forms to express *this*, *these*, *that*, *those* as adjectives:

	this, these	that, those (near you)	that, those (over there)
masc. sing.	este	ese	aquel
fem. sing.	esta	esa	aquella
masc. plur.	estos	esos	aquellos
fem. plur.	estas	esas	aquellas

Examples

Este libro es nuevo. = **This** book is new.
Mc gusta **esa** bolsa. = I like **that** bag (near you).
Hay un pájaro en **aquel** árbol. = There is a bird in **that** tree (over there).

Exercise

Put the correct form as indicated in the bracket.

a) . . . hombre es mi abuelo. (that)
b) No me gusta . . . novela. (this)
c) . . . uvas no están maduras. (those)
d) No voy nunca a . . . casa. (that – over there)
e) . . . lápices son de José. (these)

33) This one, that one, these, those, this, that, as pronouns

To translate the pronouns: *this one*, *that one*, *these*, *those*, use the same forms as the adjectives in Chapter 32, but with an accent.

	this one, these	that one, those (by you)	that one, those (over there)
masc. sing.	éste	ése	aquél
fem. sing.	ésta	ésa	aquélla
masc. plur.	éstos	ésos	aquéllos
fem. plur.	éstas	ésas	aquéllas

Examples

¿Qué bolso prefieres? **Éste.** = Which handbag do you prefer? **This one.**
¿Cuál es tu casa? **Aquélla.** = Which is your house? **That one** (over there).
¿No tienes zapatillas? Coge **ésas.** = Don't you have any slippers? Take
those (by you).

The following neuter pronouns are used, when not referring to any specific
person or thing. (Notice they do not carry an accent).
esto = this
eso = that
aquello = that

Examples

¿Qué es **esto**? = What is **this**?
Eso no es verdad. = **That** is not true.
No estoy de acuerdo con **aquello.** = I do not agree with **that.**

Exercise

Put the correct form as indicated in the brackets.

a) ¿Cuál de los libros prefieres? . . . (this one)
b) . . . son más bonitas que las otras. (these)
c) No me gusta . . . (that)
d) ¿Quieres estas manzanas? No, . . . (those)
e) . . . es lo que quiero decir. (this)

34) Todo – all, every, the whole, everything

a) **Todo** can be used as an *adjective*, and like other adjectives it matches
the noun it describes, but it is always placed in front of the noun.

Examples

todo el día = all day (long)
todos los días = every day
todo el mundo = everybody
toda Francia = the whole of France
todas sus ideas = all his ideas

b) **Todo** can be used as a *pronoun*, with **lo, la, los, las,** as appropriate before
the verb.

Examples

Lo tiene **todo**. = He has **everything**.
La han comido **toda**. = They have eaten **all of it**.
Los he leído **todos**. = I have read **all of them**.
Las hemos visto a **todas**. = We have seen **all of them** (people).

Exercise

Fill in the appropriate form of **todo**.

a) Voy a ver a mis abuelos . . . los años.
b) Las he comprado . . ..
c) Lo sabe . . ..
d) Vi a . . . la gente.

35) Comparison of adjectives – bigger, more intelligent, etc.

young = **joven**
younger = **más joven**
youngest = **el más joven**

difficult = **difícil**
more difficult = **más difícil**
most difficult = **el más difícil**

These are the masculine singular forms only, and can be made feminine and plural if necessary in the usual way. (See Chapter 28)

So you can see that:

a) **Más** = more (or **er** at the end of the adjective)
b) **El (la, los, las) más** = most (or **est** at the end of the adjective)

Examples

María es **más baja** que Pedro. = Mary is **shorter** than Peter.
Pablo es **más inteligente** que Miguel. = Paul is **more intelligent** than Michael.
Estas casas son **las más modernas** de la ciudad. = These houses are the **most modern** in the town.
Es el alumno **más tonto** de la clase. = He is the **silliest** pupil in the class

Note that **que** means **than**, and **de** means **in** with these examples.
Use **menos** to mean **less**, e.g.

Este chico es **menos inteligente** que su hermano. = This boy is **less clever** than his brother.
Mi revista es **menos interesante** que la tuya. = My magazine is **less interesting** than yours.

Use **tan** . . . **como** to mean **as** . . . **as**, e.g.

Mi madre es **tan** alta **como** yo. = My mother is **as** tall **as** me.
Juan es **tan** guapo **como** Pablo. = John is **as** handsome **as** Paul.

Special points

a) Some adjectives have special forms:

bueno = good	**mejor** = better	**el mejor** = the best
malo = bad	**peor** = worse	**el peor** = the worst

b) There are two special forms of the following adjectives depending on their meaning:

grande = big	**más grande** = bigger	**el más grande** = biggest
grande = great	**mayor** = greater, older	**el mayor** = the greatest, the oldest
pequeño = small	**más pequeño** = smaller	**el más pequeño** = the smallest
	menor = younger	**el menor** = the youngest

c) When the adjective comes after the noun, **el, la, los, las** are omitted, e.g.

La chica **más perezosa** de la clase = The **laziest** girl in the class

d) Note this special form which translates *very* . . .. It is formed by removing **o** from the end of the adjective, and adding **ísimo**, e.g.

mucho = much	**muchísimo** = very much indeed
malo = bad	**malísimo** = very bad indeed

Exercise

Fill in either **más, el (la, los, las) más**, **menos** or **tan**, followed by the adjective in the following sentences:

a) El señor Gómez es . . . que mi padre. (rico)
b) Es la chica . . . de la clase. (bonito)
c) Los chicos son . . . que las chicas. (tonto)
d) Es la iglesia . . . de la ciudad. (antiguo)
e) Son los . . . alumnos de la clase. (malo)
f) Mis hermanas son . . . como yo. (inteligente)

36) Adverbs

a) *Formation of adverbs*
Adverbs are usually formed by taking the feminine singular of the adjective,

and adding **mente**, e.g.

franca = frank	**francamente** = frankly
básica = basic	**básicamente** = basically
rápida = quick	**rápidamente** = quickly

If the feminine form of the adjective is the same as the masculine form, it does not change when **mente** is added to form the adverb, e.g.

alegre = joyful	**alegremente** = joyfully
feliz = happy	**felizmente** = happily

Some adverbs do not end in **mente**. The most common are:

bien = well, **mal** = badly, **despacio** = slowly (**lentamente** is also common)

Special points

The adverb is normally placed immediately after the verb, e.g.

El tren **sale despacio** de la estación. = The train slowly leaves the station.

If two adverbs come together you only put **mente** on the second one, e.g.

El coche va **lenta y seguramente**. = The car goes slowly and surely.

Exercise

Change the adjective in brackets into the equivalent adverb.

a) Vd. habla muy . . . español. (bueno)
b) El departamento está . . . lleno. (completo)
c) No estoy . . . satisfecho. (entero)
d) Lo ha hecho . . . (fácil)
e) El tren sale . . . de la estación. (lento)
f) Me saludó . . . (amable)

b) *Comparison of adverbs*
To do this place **más** before the adverb, e.g.

rápidamente = quickly   **más rápidamente** = more quickly

Other examples using **menos** = **less** and **tan** = **as**.

Trabaja **menos cuidadosamente** que su hermano. = He works **less carefully** than his brother.
Corre **tan rápidamente** como yo. = He runs **as quickly** as me.

Special point

Some adverbs have irregular forms.

bien = well   **mejor** = better   **lo mejor** = the best
mal = badly   **peor** = worse   **lo peor** = the worst
mucho = much   **más** = more   **lo más** = the most
poco = little   **menos** = less   **lo menos** = the least

Exercise

Fill in either **más**, **menos**, **tan** plus the adverb, or by using the appropriate irregular form.

a) Leemos . . . que Miguel. (rápidamente)
b) Baila . . . que yo. (bien)
c) Escribo . . . que mi hermano. (lentamente)
d) Trabaja . . . por la tarde. (mal)
e) Camina . . . como yo. (despacio)

37) Future tense – I shall eat, he will buy, etc.

The future tense shows what *will* happen tomorrow, next month, or some time in the future. All verbs, regular and irregular, have the same endings for the future tense.

To form the future tense, the endings given below should be added to the *infinitive* (see explanation of English terms used). Verbs which are irregular in the future tense do not use the infinitive. Check the verbs table. (See Chapter 59)

yo – é	nosotros – emos
tú – ás	vosotros – éis
él ⎫	ellos ⎫
ella ⎬ – á	ellas ⎬ – án
Vd. ⎭	Vds. ⎭

Here is an example of the future tense of a regular verb:

hablaré = I shall speak   **hablaremos** = we shall speak
hablarás = you will speak   **hablaréis** = you will speak
          (*fam. sing.*)   (*fam. plur.*)
hablará = he, she, it will speak   **hablarán** = they will speak
Vd. hablará = you will speak   **Vds. hablarán** = you will speak
          (*pol. sing.*)   (*pol. plur.*)

Here are some examples of the use of the future tense:

Compraré un coche. = **I shall buy** a car.
Comerá un bocadillo. = **He will eat** a sandwich.
Recibirán muchos regalos. = **They will receive** a lot of presents.

Exercise

Put the verb in **bold print** into the future tense.

a) Mi madre **prepara** la comida.
b) **Bebo** una cerveza.
c) El chico se **baña** en el lago.
d) **Escribimos** muchas cartas.
e) **Trabajan** en una tienda.
f) ¿Dónde **vives**?
g) Se **levantan** muy tarde.

38) Talking about the future using ir a plus the infinitive.

An immediate future can be formed by using the present tense of **ir** = **to go** (see Chapter 59) as the main verb. This gives the idea of *going to do* in English. The correct part of **ir** is used to match the subject of the sentence. It is followed by **a** and the second verb always remains in the infinitive.

Examples

Voy a comprar un periódico. = **I am going to buy** a newspaper.
Van a ir al cine. = **They are going to go** to the cinema.
Vamos a coger el tren. = **We are going to catch** the train.

Exercise

Put the verbs in **bold print** into the future by using **ir a** and the infinitive.

a) **Hablo** con mi abuela.
b) Pablo **vende** sus discos.
c) Se **lavan** en el cuarto de baño.
d) **Vivimos** en Barcelona.
e) ¿Qué **haces**?

39) Object pronouns

Direct object

me = me
te = you (*fam. sing.*)
le { him
        you (*masculine pol. sing.*)
la { her
        you (*feminine pol. sing.*)
lo = it (*masculine*)
la = it (*feminine*)
nos = us
os = you (*fam. plur.*)
les { them (*masculine – people*)
         you (*masculine pol. plur.*)
las { them (*feminine – people*)
         you (*feminine pol. plur.*)
los = them (*masculine – things*)
las = them (*feminine – things*)

Occasionally **lo** meaning **him** and **los** meaning **them** (*masculine – people*) are found.

Indirect object

me = to me
te = to you (*fam. sing.*)
le = to him, to her, to you (*pol. sing.*)
nos = to us
os = to you (*fam. plur.*)
les = to them, to you (*pol. plur.*)

In English the object pronouns are placed after the verb, e.g. I saw *him*, we met *her*, he talked *to me*, etc. In Spanish the object pronouns are placed immediately *before* the verb. (For the exceptions to this rule see **Special points**, a–c below.)

Examples

He sees **us**. = **Nos** ve.
They talk **to me**. = **Me** hablan.
We write **to them**. = **Les** escribimos.

Special points

The object pronoun is tacked on to the end of the verb in the following three cases:

a) Infinitive, e.g.

Vienen a **verme**. = They are coming **to see me**.

b) Present participle, e.g.

Estudiándolo. = **Studying it**. (Note the accent)

c) Command which is not negative (see Chapter 40), e.g.

Espéreme. = **Wait for me**. (Note the accent)

When two object pronouns, one direct, one indirect, are together, the indirect always goes before the direct, e.g.

Va a dár**melo**. = He is going to give it to me.
Me lo ha prestado. = He has lent it to me.

When **le** or **les** comes before **lo, la, los** or **las**, you must change the **le** or **les** to **se**, e.g.

Se lo enseño. = I show it to him.
No quiero dár**selo**. = I don't want to give it to him.

Because in this case **se** can mean *to him*, *to her*, *to you* (*polite*), *to them* it is common to add **a él, a ella, a Vd., a ellos, a ellas, a Vds.** to make the sense clear, e.g.

Voy a prestár**selo a él**. = I am going to lend it to him.
Voy a prestár**selo a Vd**. = I am going to lend it to you.

Note that an accent is required on the ending of the infinitive when two object pronouns are added. (See Chapter 58)

When two verbs come together and the second one is in the infinitive, pronouns can be put in front of the first verb, or tacked on to the end of the infinitive, e.g.

Se la voy a dar. *or* Voy a dár**sela**. = I am going to give it to him.

Similarly with the continuous tenses pronouns can be put in front of the part of **estar** or tacked on to the end of the present participle, e.g.

Se los estoy mandando. *or* Estoy mandándo**selos**. = I am sending them to her.

Exercise

Replace the words in **bold print** with object pronouns.

a) Voy a mandar **el regalo a mis tíos**.

b) Me ha prestado **sus gafas**.
c) No quiero darla **a mi hermano**.
d) Compramos **las uvas** en esa tienda.
e) He buscado **el perro** por todas partes.

40) Commands and object pronouns

In a command the object pronouns are tacked on to the end of the verb if the command is *to do* something. The pronouns go before the verb if the command is *not to do* something, e.g.

Escríbanos. = **Write to us**.
No nos escriba. = **Don't write to us**.
Cuéntemelo. = **Tell me it**.
No me lo cuente. = **Don't tell me it**.

Note an accent is required if an object pronoun is put on the end of the command.

Exercise

Change the words in **bold print** into object pronouns.

a) Muestre **los zapatos a mi amigo**.
b) No dé **el libro a los niños**.
c) Busque **las postales**.
d) No pase **la mantequilla a María**.

41) Strong pronouns

mí = me	**nosotros** = us
ti = you (*fam. sing.*)	**vosotros** = you (*fam. plur.*)
él = him, it	**ellos** = them (*masc.*)
ella = her, it	**ellas** = them (*fem.*)
Vd. = you (*pol. sing.*)	**Vds.** = you (*pol. plur.*)
sí = oneself, etc.	

Strong pronouns are *not* the same as object pronouns, and should only be used after prepositions, e.g.

sin mí = without me
con él = with him
para ellos = for them

Special points

Sí means *himself, herself, yourself (polite), themselves, oneself* when **sí** refers back to the subject of the sentence, e.g.

Habla para **sí**. = He talks to **himself**.

Note the special forms **conmigo** = with me, **contigo** = with you (*fam. sing.*), and **consigo** = with him(self) etc., e.g.

Lo ha llevado **consigo**. = He has taken it with him.

Exercise

Put a strong pronoun to translate the word in brackets.

a) Este regalo es para . . . (you – *fam. sing.*)
b) Va Vd. a llevarlo con . . . (you)
c) Mi hermano ha salido con . . . (her)
d) No quiero hablar delante de . . . (them)
e) ¿Por qué no vienes con . . . ? (me)
f) Lo he hecho por . . . (you – *pol. sing.*)
g) Se han marchado sin . . . (us)

42) Preterite (past) tense – I spoke, he arrived, etc.

The preterite tense, also called the *simple past*, is mainly used to describe an action which has ended in the past, or an action in the past that we cannot repeat. It translates 'he wrote', 'she listened' etc., unlike the perfect tense (Chapter 44), which translates 'he has written', 'she has listened'. For example:

Ayer compré una corbata. = Yesterday I bought a tie.

That particular 'yesterday' cannot be repeated, and so the preterite tense is used.

a) *Regular ar verbs*

To form the preterite tense of these verbs, remove the **ar** from the infinitive, and add the following endings:

yo – é	**nosotros – amos**
tú – aste	**vosotros – asteis**
él ⎫	**ellos** ⎫
ella ⎬ **– ó**	**ellas** ⎬ **– aron**
Vd. ⎭	**Vds.** ⎭

Here is an example of the preterite tense of a regular **ar** verb:

tomé = I took   **tomamos** = we took
tomaste = you took (*fam. sing.*)   **tomasteis** = you took (*fam. plur.*)
tomó = he, she, it took   **tomaron** = they took
Vd. tomó = you took (*pol. sing.*)   **Vds. tomaron** = you took (*pol. plur.*)

Here are some examples of the use of the preterite tense:

Esta mañana **tomé** un taxi. = This morning I **took** a taxi.
Se **levantó** a las nueve. = He **got up** at nine o'clock.

b) *Regular er and ir verbs*

To form the preterite tense of these verbs, remove the **er** or **ir** from the infinitive and add the following endings:

yo – í	**nosotros – imos**
tú – iste	**vosotros – isteis**
él ⎫	**ellos** ⎫
ella ⎬ **– ió**	**ellas** ⎬ **– ieron**
Vd. ⎭	**Vds.** ⎭

Here is an example of the preterite tense of a regular **er** verb:

bebí = I drank   **bebimos** = we drank
bebiste = you drank (*fam. sing.*)   **bebisteis** = you drank (*fam. plur.*)
bebió = he, she, it drank   **bebieron** = they drank
Vd. bebió = you drank   **Vds. bebieron** = you drank
          (*pol. sing.*)   (*pol. plur.*)

Here are some examples of the use of the preterite tense:

Comimos muchos caramelos. = We **ate** a lot of sweets.
Escribieron una carta a sus padres. = They **wrote** a letter to their parents.

Exercise

Put the verbs in **bold print** into the preterite.

a) María **habla** con el profesor.
b) **Bebo** vino en el restaurante.
c) Vds. **reciben** muchos regalos.
d) ¿Qué **comes**?
e) **Llegamos** a las once.

43) Special preterites

a) Some verbs have an irregular preterite form; nevertheless they do follow a pattern. They are often referred to as *stressed preterites*. Here are their endings:

yo – e	**nosotros – imos**
tú – iste	**vosotros – isteis**
él ⎫	**ellos** ⎫
ella ⎬ **– o**	**ellas** ⎬ **– ieron**
Vd. ⎭	**Vds.** ⎭

Special points

These verbs do not use the infinitive to form the preterite tense, but add the endings to another stem which must be learned separately.

Note that there are no accents on these endings.

Here is an example of a special preterite:

tuve = I had	**tuvimos** = we had
tuviste = you had (*fam. sing.*)	**tuvisteis** = you had (*fam. plur.*)
tuvo = he, she, it had	**tuvieron** = they had
Vd. tuvo = you had (*pol. sing.*)	**Vds. tuvieron** = you had (*pol. plur.*)

Here is a list of the most common stressed preterites:

andar = to walk	**anduve**
conducir = to drive	**conduje (condujeron)**
decir = to say, tell	**dije (dijeron)**
estar = to be	**estuve**
hacer = to do, make	**hice (hizo)**

obtener = to obtain   **obtuve**
poder = to be able   **pude**
poner = to put   **puse**
producir = to produce   **produje (produjeron)**
querer = to wish, want   **quise**
saber = to know   **supe**
suponer = to suppose   **supuse**
tener = to have   **tuve**
traer = to bring   **traje (trajeron)**
venir = to come   **vine**

b) There are three verbs which have to be learned individually because they do not belong to either the regular preterites or the stressed preterites.

dar = to give

di   **dimos**
diste   **disteis**
dio   **dieron**
Vd. dio   Vds. dieron

ser = to be   and   **ir** = to go

fui   **fuimos**
fuiste   **fuisteis**
fue   **fueron**
Vd. fue   Vds. fueron

These two verbs have exactly the same form in the preterite tense, but because they have such different meanings they are not confused, e.g.

Mi hermano **fue** al mercado = My brother **went** to the market.
Mi hermano **fue** profesor = My brother **was** a teacher.

Exercise

Put the verb in brackets into the correct form of the preterite tense.

a) Vd. . . . las manzanas a su hijo. (dar)
b) (Ellos) . . . al partido de fútbol. (ir)
c) (Yo) . . . dos años en Francia. (estar)
d) (Nosotros) . . . los vasos sobre la mesa. (poner)
e) ¿ . . . (tú) a verme? (venir)

44) Perfect (past) tense

The perfect tense shows an action that has happened in the past, but which can be repeated in the present or future. It is formed by using the present tense of **haber**, followed by the past participle of the main verb. For example:

He comprado una corbata en París. = I have bought a tie in Paris.

(Implies that you can go to Paris some time in the future and can buy a tie there again.)

Present tense of **haber**:

he = I have	**hemos** = we have
has = you have (*fam. sing.*)	**habéis** = you have (*fam. plur.*)
ha = he, she, it has	**han** = they have
Vd. ha = you have (*pol. sing.*)	**Vds. han** = you have (*pol. plur.*)

The past participle is formed with **ar** verbs by taking off the **ar** and putting **ado**. With **er** and **ir** verbs it is formed by taking off the **er** or **ir** and putting **ido**.

hablar – hablado
comer – comido
vivir – vivido

Here is an example of a regular **ar** verb in the perfect tense:

he hablado = I have spoken
has hablado = you have spoken (*fam. sing.*)
ha hablado = he, she, it has spoken
Vd. ha hablado = you have spoken (*pol. sing.*)
hemos hablado = we have spoken
habéis hablado = you have spoken (*fam. plur.*)
han hablado = they have spoken
Vds. han hablado = you have spoken (*pol. plur.*)

Here is an example of a regular **er** verb in the perfect tense:

he comido = I have eaten
has comido = you have eaten (*fam. sing.*)
etc.

Here is an example of a regular **ir** verb in the perfect tense:

he vivido = I have lived
has vivido = you have lived (*fam. sing.*)
etc.

There are some past participles which do not follow the rules, and these must be carefully learned. The most common can be found in the irregular verbs table in Chapter 59. Others are: **abierto** = opened, **cubierto** = covered, **escrito** = written, **roto** = broken, **vuelto** = returned.

Special points

Object and reflexive pronouns are placed immediately before the part of **haber**, e.g.

Se lo he dado. = I have given **it to him**.

To make the perfect tense negative, put **no** in front of the part of **haber**, or in front of the object or reflexive pronoun, if there is one, e.g.

No he dado el libro a Juan. = I **haven't** given the book to John.
No se lo he dado. = I **haven't** given **it** to him.

If **Vd.** or **Vds.** appear in a question in the perfect tense they are placed after the past participle, e.g.

¿Le ha **visto Vd.**? = Have you seen him?

Note that the part of **haber** must never be separated from the past participle by any other word, e.g.

No le **he encontrado** nunca. = I have never met him.

Exercise

Put the words in **bold print** into the perfect tense.

a) **Estamos** en Londres.
b) ¿Qué le **dices**?
c) ¿Quién **rompe** el florero?
d) **Van** a Francia este año.
e) ¿**Veis** el partido?
f) No **tengo** tiempo.
g) ¿Cuándo **escribe** Vd. la carta?
h) No **hago** nada.

45) Acabar de, desde and desde hace

These constructions have meanings in English in the past tense, but use the present or imperfect tense (see Chapter 46) in Spanish, *never* the perfect tense.

Acabar de = **to have just** (done something), using the present tense. The second verb must be in the *infinitive*. To express **had just**, use the imperfect tense.

Examples

Acaba de llegar. = **He has just arrived.**
Acabábamos de telefonear. = We had just telephoned.

Exercise

Answer the following questions, putting the correct form of the verb to match the subject, e.g.

Acabo de terminar. ¿Y José?
José **acaba de terminar.**

a) Acaba de hallar el dinero. ¿Y los chicos?
b) Acabamos de comer. ¿Y tú?
c) Acaban de lavarse. ¿Y vosotros?

Desde = since

Example

Buscan una casa **desde** diciembre. = **They have been looking** for a house **since** December.

Desde hace = for

Example

Estudio español **desde hace** dos años. = **I have been studying** Spanish **for** two years.

Another way of saying the same thing:
Hace dos años **que** estudio español.

Notice also the way in which the question is formed:

¿Desde cuándo vive Vd. aquí? ⎫ How long have you been living
¿Cuánto tiempo hace que vive Vd. aquí?⎭ here?

Exercise

Answer the following questions, putting the correct form of the verb to match the subject, e.g.

Vive aquí desde hace un mes. ¿Y Pedro?
Pedro **vive** aquí **desde hace** un mes.

a) Juego al tenís desde hace una hora. ¿Y las chicas?
b) Trabajo con ellos desde hace cinco años. ¿Y vosotros?
c) Ve la televisión desde hace diez minutos. ¿Y tú?
d) Viven en Inglaterra desde enero. ¿Y Vds.?

46) The imperfect tense

The imperfect tense is used to express something which *was happening* or *used to happen*, or for *description* of a continuous action in the past. There are two sets of endings, one for **ar** verbs and another for **er** and **ir** verbs.

ar verb endings

yo – aba	nosotros – ábamos
tú – abas	vosotros – ábais
él ⎫	ellos ⎫
ella ⎬ – aba	ellas ⎬ – aban
Vd. ⎭	Vds. ⎭

Here is an example of a regular **ar** verb in the imperfect tense.

hablaba = I was talking, I used to talk
hablabas = you were talking, you used to talk (*fam. sing.*)
hablaba = he, she, it was talking, used to talk
Vd. hablaba = you were talking, you used to talk (*pol. sing.*)
hablábamos = we were talking, we used to talk
hablábais = you were talking, you used to talk (*fam. plur.*)
hablaban = they were talking, they used to talk
Vds. hablaban = you were talking, you used to talk (*pol. plur.*)

er and **ir** endings

yo – ía	nosotros – íamos
tú – ías	vosotros – íais
él ⎫	ellos ⎫
ella ⎬ – ía	ellas ⎬ – ían
Vd. ⎭	Vds. ⎭

Here is an example of a regular **er** verb in the imperfect tense.

comía = I was eating, I used to eat
comías = you were eating, you used to eat
etc.

Here is an example of a regular **ir** verb in the imperfect tense.

vivía = I was living, I used to live
vivías = you were living, you used to live
etc.

Irregular imperfects

ser = to be

era	**éramos**
eras	**érais**
era	**eran**
Vd. era	**Vds. eran**

ir = to go

iba	**íbamos**
ibas	**íbais**
iba	**iban**
Vd. iba	**Vds. iban**

ver = to see

veía	**veíamos**
veías	**veíais**
veía	**veían**
Vd. veía	**Vds. veían**

Examples

Era muy joven = He **was** very young
Lo **hacía** todos los días. = He **used to do** it every day.
Cuando **estaba** en Londres **trabajaba** mucho. = When he **was** in London he used to work very hard.

Special points

To express *was . . . ing* the continuous form can be used in the imperfect tense. Use the imperfect form of **estar**, followed by the present participle. There is virtually no difference in meaning between the two forms, e.g.

Llovía = It **was raining**
Estaba lloviendo = It **was raining**

Note that although they are both past tenses there is a difference between the imperfect and the preterite. The imperfect tense is used to express an action which was going on, or a description, and the preterite is used to express an action which came to interrupt it, e.g.

Llovía cuando **salí.** = It **was raining** when I **went out.**
Mientras **trabajaba tomé** un vaso de vino. = While I **was working** I **had** a glass of wine.
Dormía cuando alguien **llamó** a la puerta. = I **was sleeping** when there **was** a knock on the door.

There can be no confusion between the perfect and imperfect tenses because they are translated into English in quite different ways.

Example

Perfect tense: Ha **escrito** una carta. = He **has written** a letter.
Imperfect tense: **Escribía** una carta. = He **was writing** a letter.

Exercise

Change the word in **bold print** into the imperfect tense.

a) **Voy** al parque todos los domingos.
b) Le **ve** muchas veces en Madrid.
c) **Nieva** en el invierno.
d) **Hace** mucho calor en agosto.
e) **Trabaja** de nueve a una.
f) **Son** niños muy traviesos.

47) Pluperfect tense – I had bought, we had made, etc.

The pluperfect tense shows what *had* happened, or what someone *had* done in the past. It is formed with the imperfect tense of the verb **haber** followed by the past participle of the main verb.

Here is an example of the pluperfect tense of a regular verb, **hablar** = to speak:

había hablado = I had spoken
habías hablado = you had spoken (*fam. sing.*)
había hablado = he, she, it had spoken
Vd. había hablado = you had spoken (*pol. sing.*)
habíamos hablado = we had spoken
habíais hablado = you had spoken (*fam. plur.*)
habían hablado = they had spoken
Vds. habían hablado = you had spoken (*pol. plur.*)

Some examples of the usage of the pluperfect tense:

Habías terminado tus deberes. = **You had finished** your homework.
(Yo) había bebido la limonada. = **I had drunk** the lemonade.
Habíamos recibido muchas cartas. = **We had received** a lot of letters.

The rules for negatives, object and reflexive pronouns, irregular past participles and word order are the same as in the perfect tense (see Chapter 44).

Exercise

Change the verb in brackets into the correct form of the pluperfect tense.

a) Pablo . . . en el cuarto de baño. (lavarse)
b) (Yo) . . . dos pasteles. (comer)
c) Vds. . . . postales a sus hijas. (escribir)
d) (Nosotros) . . . en Sevilla. (vivir)
e) ¿ . . . Vd. la ventana? (abrir)

48) Conditional tense – I should like, he would go, etc.

The conditional tense shows what *should* or *would* happen, or what someone *should* or *would* do. All the verbs have the same endings for the conditional tense, and these are added to the infinitive in the same way as the future tense is formed (see Chapter 37).

Here are the endings:

yo – ía	nosotros – íamos	
tú – ías	vosotros – íais	
él	ellos	
ella } – ía	ellas } – ían	
Vd.	Vds.	

Here is an example of the conditional tense of a regular verb, **comer** = to eat:

comería = I should eat
comerías = you would eat (*fam. sing.*)
comería = he, she, it would eat
Vd. comería = you would eat (*pol. sing.*)
comeríamos = we would eat
comeríais = you would eat (*fam. plur.*)
comerían = they would eat
Vds. comerían = you would eat (*pol. plur.*)

Some examples of usage of the conditional tense:

Compraría un coche. = I **would buy** a car.
Beberían mucho vino. = They **would drink** a lot of wine.
Viviría en Madrid. = He **would live** in Madrid.

Special points

a) Irregular verbs have the same endings as regular verbs in this tense. The irregularity occurs in the stem exactly as in the future tense. Check irregular verbs table (Chapter 59).

b) The conditional tense of **gustar** is very useful, e.g.

Me **gustaría** ir al cine. = I **would like** to go to the cinema.
Le **gustaría** a Juan comprar un coche. = John **would like** to buy a car.

Exercise

Put the verbs in **bold print** into the conditional tense.

a) Pablo **va** a Londres.
b) **Hablo** con el jefe.
c) Vds. **escriben** un libro.
d) Me **gusta** ver la televisión.
e) ¿Qué **bebes**?

49) Relative pronouns

The word for *who*, *whom*, *which* and *that* is **que**. Sometimes *whom* is expressed as **a quien** (*singular*) or **a quienes** (*plural*), e.g.

El hombre **que** lleva gafas. = The man **who** wears glasses.
La chica **que** (**a quien**) viste es mi hermana. = The girl (**whom**) you saw is my sister.
La caja **que** está sobre la mesa es mía. = The box **which** is on the table is mine.
¿Es éste el libro **que** perdiste? = Is this the book **that** you lost?

Although the words *whom*, *which* and *that* are often missed out in English, **que** must never be missed out in Spanish, e.g.

That is the girl I met yesterday. = Ésa es la chica **que** encontré ayer.
Here is the dress I bought this morning. = Aquí está el vestido **que** compré esta mañana.

Use **quien** to translate *whom* after prepositions, e.g.

> Allí está el hombre **a quien** di la carta. = There is the man **to whom** I gave the letter.
>
> ¿Conoces al chico **con quien** sale? = Do you know the boy she is going out with?

Special point

Cuyo, a, os, as means *whose* when not in a question. It agrees with the word which follows it, e.g.

> El hombre **cuya** casa está en venta no ha venido. = The man **whose** house is for sale has not come.

Exercise

Fill in **que, quien** or **cuyo, a, os, as**, as appropriate.

a) Deme las gafas . . . están sobre la mesa.
b) Allí está el chico . . . hermana se casó con mi hijo.
c) ¿Es éste el hombre de . . . hablabas?
d) Los amigos . . . van a venir son españoles.

50) El que, el cual, etc.

The word *which* after a preposition can be translated in the following ways:

el que, la que, los que, las que
or
el cual, la cual, los cuales, las cuales.

The form used must match the noun to which it refers, e.g.

> La regla **con la que** (**con la cual**) jugaba. = The ruler he was playing with.

Special points

A, en or **de** can be followed simply by **que**, e.g.

> ¿Dónde está el libro **de que** hablabas? = Where is the book you were talking about?

Lo que translates *what* in the middle of a sentence, e.g.

> Quiero saber **lo que** estás haciendo. = I want to know what you are doing.

Exercise

Fill in the appropriate part of **el que**, **el cual**, etc.

a) Aquí están los huevos sobre . . . estaba sentado.
b) Deme el lápiz con . . . dibujabas.
c) ¿Conoces el colegio detrás de . . . hay un bosque grande?
d) La casa al lado de . . . hay un supermercado es mía.

51) The present subjunctive

The present subjunctive is a form of the verb which is used in certain expressions and also in some commands (see Chapter 23).

It is formed in the following way.

Ar verbs:

Take the **yo** part of the present tense, remove the **o** and add the following endings:

yo – e	nosotros – emos
tú – es	vosotros – éis
él	ellos
ella } – e	ellas } – en
Vd.	Vds.

Here is an example:

hable	**hablemos**
hables	**habléis**
hable	**hablen**
Vd. hable	**Vds. hablen**

Er and **Ir** verbs:

Take the **yo** part of the present tense, remove the **o** and add the following endings:

yo – a	nosotros – amos
tú – as	vosotros – áis
él	ellos
ella } – a	ellas } – an
Vd.	Vds.

Here is an example:

escriba	**escribamos**
escribas	**escribáis**
escriba	**escriban**
Vd. escriba	**Vds. escriban**

The irregular forms of the present subjunctive can be found in the irregular verbs table (Chapter 59).

There are many occasions when the present subjunctive is required. If you want to know all the usages you must consult a more detailed grammar book. However, the most common uses are the following:

a) After a verb of *wanting someone to do something*. The word **que** must be used in the sentence, and two different subjects, one on either side of the **que**, must be used. For example:

Quiero que **venga**. = I want **him to come**. (Literally, I want that **he comes**.)

b) After a verb expressing *emotion*. The use of **que** and two subjects occurs here as well. For example:

Siento que no **haya venido**. = I am sorry **he has not come**.

c) After a verb of *command, telling or asking someone to do something*. The use of **que** and two subjects occurs here as well. For example:

Dile que **venga** a verme. = Tell **him to come** and see me. (Literally, Tell him that **he comes** to see me.)

d) After certain *impersonal* expressions, for example, *it is necessary*, *it is possible*, *it is probable*, *it is impossible*, etc. Many of these expressions show *uncertainty* or *doubt*. For example:

Es posible que **sepa** la verdad. = It is possible that **he knows** the truth.

e) After **cuando** when followed by a *future idea*, for example:

Comeremos cuando mi padre **llegue**. = We will eat when my father **arrives**.

Exercise

Put the verb in brackets into the correct form of the present subjunctive.

a) Es posible que (él) lo . . . mañana. (hacer)
b) Dígale que . . . la ventana. (cerrar)
c) Voy a preparar la cena cuando (ellos) . . . (venir)
d) ¿Quieres que (yo) . . . la puerta? (abrir)
e) Le pediré que . . . en la estación de servicio. (detenerse)

52) Si – if (followed by the present tense)

The future tense must not be used in Spanish with **si**, even if the meaning sometimes suggests a future time. Use the present tense as in English, e.g.

Si viene, iremos al cine. = **If he comes**, we will go to the cinema.
Si termino a tiempo, iré contigo. = **If I finish** in time, I will go with you.

Exercise

Fill in the correct form of the verb given in brackets.

a) Si (nosotros) . . . a Madrid, visitaremos el Rastro. (ir)
b) Si (yo) . . . temprano, prepararé la comida. (llegar)
c) Si (tú) . . . demasiado chocolate, estarás enfermo. (comer)
d) Si (él) . . . mucho dinero, te dará cien pesetas. (recibir)

53) Sentarse and estar sentado

The verb **sentarse** means **to sit down** and describes the action of someone in the process of sitting down. The verb **estar sentado** means **to be seated** or **sitting**, and describes the state of someone who has already sat down.

Examples

a) He is sitting in the car. This describes the state of being seated, so use **estar sentado**.
Está sentado en el coche.
b) She sat down quickly. This describes the action of sitting down, so use **sentarse**.
Se sentó de prisa.
c) We are going to sit down now. This describes the action of sitting down, so use **sentarse**.
Vamos a **sentarnos** ahora.

Special points

Sentarse is a radical changing verb. (See Chapter 55)

Estar sentado follows the pattern of **estar**, but **sentado** is an adjective and so has to match the subject of the sentence, e.g.

Las chicas **están sentadas**. = The girls **are sitting down**.

Exercise

Fill in the correct form of either **sentarse** or **estar sentado**.

a) María . . . en el comedor. (is sitting)
b) (Nosotros) . . . en la playa. (sit down)
c) Los chicos . . . ahora. (sit down)
d) ¿Vas a . . . ?
e) (Yo) . . . en el salón. (am sitting)

54) The passive

The passive gives the idea of an action *being done* to someone or something.

It is formed by using **ser** or **estar** with the past participle. You use *estar* to express a *state*, and **ser** to express an *action*, e.g.

The door **is closed**. (*state*) = La puerta **está cerrada**.
The door **is closed** by John. (*action*) = La puerta **es cerrada** por Juan.

Note that the past participle is acting as an adjective, and must match the subject.

By is translated by **por** in a passive sentence.

In the past, there are four possible ways of translating *was* or *were*, depending on whether it is a state or an action, and whether it happened once or continuously. Study these examples:

El soldado **fue** fusilado. = The soldier **was** shot.
Los árboles **eran** cortados todos los años. = The trees **were** cut every year.
Las tiendas **estuvieron** cerradas toda la semana. = The shops **were** shut for the whole week.
Las tiendas **estaban** cerradas cuando llegamos. = The shops **were** shut when we arrived.

Special point

The passive is often avoided in Spanish in the following ways:
1) Use the impersonal pronoun **se** instead, e.g.

Spanish is spoken here. → Spanish speaks itself here. → Aquí **se habla** español. (Note that **español** is the subject of the verb, so the verb must match it.)

2) If the person or thing doing the action is mentioned, turn the sentence round, e.g.

He was killed by a bullet. → A bullet killed him. → **Una bala le mató.**

3) Put the verb in the *they* form, which makes it sound indefinite, e.g.

The horses were brought to market. → They brought the horses to market. → **Trajeron** los caballos al mercado.

Exercise

i) Change the following sentences into the passive:

a) Mandaron las cartas.
b) El coche atropelló al niño.
c) Se cerró la puerta.

ii) Avoid the passive in the following sentences:

a) El equipaje fue facturado.
b) Los pasaportes fueron examinados.
c) El silbido fue oído.

55) Radical changing verbs in all tenses

a) *Group I*

e changes to **ie**
o changes to **ue**

This change occurs in all parts of the present tense, except the **nosotros** and **vosotros** forms, (see Chapter 18), and in the same parts of the present subjunctive. (See Chapter 51) Note this change also occurs in the **tú, Vd.** and **Vds.** commands. (See Chapter 23)

b) *Group II* (All verbs in this group are **ir** verbs.)

e changes to **ie**
o changes to **ue**

This change occurs as in Group I, and in addition in the present subjunctive **e** changes to **i** and **o** changes to **u** in the **nosotros** and **vosotros** forms.

Examples

sentir = to feel

present tense		*present subjunctive*	
siento	sentimos	sienta	sintamos
sientes	sentís	sientas	sintáis
siente	sienten	sienta	sientan
Vd. siente	Vds. sienten	Vd. sienta	Vds. sientan

dormir = to sleep

present tense		*present subjunctive*	
duermo	dormimos	duerma	durmamos
duermes	dormís	duermas	durmáis
duerme	duermen	duerma	duerman
Vd. duerme	Vds. duermen	Vd. duerma	Vds. duerman

Also   e changes to **i** ⎱ in the present participle
         o changes to **u** ⎰

Examples

sintiendo   durmiendo

Also

In the preterite **él, ella, Vd., ellos, ellas, Vds.** forms:
   e changes to **i**
   o changes to **u**

Examples

Preterite tense of **sentir**

sentí	sentimos
sentiste	sentisteis
sintió	sintieron
Vd. sintió	Vds. sintieron

Preterite tense of **dormir**

dormí	dormimos
dormiste	dormisteis
durmió	durmieron
Vd. durmió	Vds. durmieron

c) *Group III* (All verbs in this group are **ir** verbs.)

   e changes to **i**

This change occurs in the same parts of the present tense as in Groups I and II, but in all parts of the present subjunctive **e** changes to **i**.

Example

pedir = to ask for

present tense		*present subjunctive*	
pido	pedimos	pida	pidamos
pides	pedís	pidas	pidáis
pide	piden	pida	pidan
Vd. pide	Vds. piden	Vd. pida	Vds. pidan

Also: **e** changes to **i** in the present participle.

Example

pidiendo

Also: **e** changes to **i** in the preterite tense as in Group II.

Example

Preterite tense of **pedir**

pedí	pedimos
pediste	pedisteis
pidió	pidieron
Vd. pidió	Vds. pidieron

Exercise

Put the verb in brackets into the correct form of the appropriate tense.

a) Los niños . . . de sus padres ayer. (despedirse)
b) No grites. Los abuelos están . . . (dormir)
c) (Ellos) no . . . nunca la puerta. (cerrar)
d) (Yo) no . . . mal ahora. (sentirse)
e) Cuando fue al restaurante . . . churros. (pedir)

56) Parts of the body – a reference list

ankle	= **el tobillo**	chin	= **la barbilla**
arm	= **el brazo**	ear	= **la oreja**
back	= **las espaldas**	elbow	= **el codo**
body	= **el cuerpo**	eye	= **el ojo**
cheek	= **la mejilla**	face	= **el rostro, la cara**
chest	= **el pecho**	finger	= **el dedo**

foot	= **el pie**		neck	= **el cuello**
forehead	= **la frente**		nose	= **la nariz**
hair	= **el pelo**		shoulder	= **el hombro**
hand	= **la mano**		skin	= **la piel**
head	= **la cabeza**		stomach	= **el estómago**
heel	= **el talón**		thigh	= **el muslo**
hip	= **la cadera**		thumb	= **el pulgar**
knee	= **la rodilla**		toe	= **el dedo del pie**
leg	= **la pierna**		tongue	= **la lengua**
lip	= **el labio**		tooth	÷ **el diente**
mouth	= **la boca**		waist	= **la cintura**
nail	= **la uña**		wrist	= **la muñeca**

57) Spelling changes

Because of the rules of Spanish spelling, some changes are required on certain occasions, particularly with verbs.
Here are examples of the most important changes:

a) **z** changes to **c** when followed by **e** or **i**, e.g.

Empecé a llorar. = I began to cry.

(All verbs ending in **zar** in the infinitive have this change.)

b) **g** (pronounced like **g** in goat) changes to **gu** when followed by **e** or **i**, e.g.

Jugué al tenis. = I played at tennis.

(All verbs ending in **gar** in the infinitive have this change.)

c) **c** (pronounced like **c** in cake) changes to **qu** when followed by **e** or **i**, e.g.

Busqué a mi madre. = I looked for my mother.

(All verbs ending in **car** in the infinitive have this change.)

d) When verbs whose infinitive ends in **ger** have an ending which does not begin with **e** or **i**, change the **g** to **j**, e.g.

Coja la pelota. = Catch the ball.

e) When verbs whose infinitive ends in **guir** have an ending not beginning with **e** or **i**, change **gu** to **g**, e.g.

Siga Vd. hablando. = Carry on talking.

f) With the following verbs, **creer**, **leer**, **oír**, **construir**, **destruir**, **caer**, in the **él, ella, Vd., ellos, ellas** and **Vds.** forms of the preterite and in the present participle, change **i** to **y**, e.g.

Cayó al río. = He fell in the river.
Oyeron la música. = They heard the music.

Exercise

Put the verb in brackets into the correct form as appropriate.

a) Siempre (yo) . . . el autobús. (coger)
b) (Yo) . . . anoche. (llegar)
c) Cuando los coches se pararon (yo) . . . la calle. (cruzar)
d) ¡ . . . Vds. el ejercicio! (empezar)
e) Los chicos están . . . el periódico. (leer)

58) Accents

a) The mark which is sometimes found over an **n** is called a **tilde** and is used to change the sound to *ny*, e.g.

señor,   España

b) The only other accent in Spanish is:
Use the following rules when deciding whether to put an accent:
a) If the word ends in a vowel, or **n** or **s**, the stress is naturally on the *last bu: one* syllable, and no accent is required, e.g.

hablando, joven, bombones

b) If the word ends in a consonant (apart from **n** or **s**), the stress is naturally on the *last* syllable, and no accent is required, e.g.

Madrid, reloj, feliz, azul, vivir

c) If the pronunciation of the word breaks either of the two rules above, an accent is placed over the vowel which requires the stress, e.g.

América, avión, jóvenes, inglés, habló

Other reasons for using an accent:
a) With question words such as *Who?*, *Why?*, *Where?* etc. which should be written as: ¿**Quién?**, ¿**Por qué?**, ¿**Dónde?** etc.

b) To show the difference between two words which have the same spelling but different meanings, e.g.

sí = yes, **si** = if; **tú** = you, **tu** = your; **sé** = I know, **se** = oneself, etc.; **dé** = give, **de** = of; **él** = he, **el** = the; **aún** = still, yet, **aun** = even.

Exercise

Put an accent if necessary on the following words.

fenomenal, cantidad, palido, contestacion, adios, fantastico, periodico, ingleses, corazon.

59) Irregular verbs table

Verb	Participles	Commands (tú & vosotros)	Present	Future	Preterite	Present Subjunctive
andar to walk	andando andado	anda andad	ando andas anda andamos andáis andan	andaré andarás andará andaremos andaréis andarán	anduve anduviste anduvo anduvimos anduvisteis anduvieron	ande andes ande andemos andéis anden
caer to fall	cayendo caído	cae caed	caigo caes cae caemos caéis caen	caeré caerás caerá caeremos caeréis caerán	caí caíste cayó caímos caísteis cayeron	caiga caigas caiga caigamos caigáis caigan
conducir to drive	conduciendo conducido	conduce conducid	conduzco conduces conduce conducimos conducís conducen	conduciré conducirás conducirá conduciremos conduciréis conducirán	conduje condujiste condujo condujimos condujisteis condujeron	conduzca conduzcas conduzca conduzcamos conduzcáis conduzcan
dar to give	dando dado	da dad	doy das da damos dais dan	daré darás dará daremos daréis darán	di diste dio dimos disteis dieron	dé des dé demos deis den

Verb	Participles	Commands (tú & vosotros)	Present	Future	Preterite	Present Subjunctive
decir to say, to tell	diciendo dicho	di decid	digo dices dice decimos decís dicen	diré dirás dirá diremos diréis dirán	dije dijiste dijo dijimos dijisteis dijeron	diga digas diga digamos digáis digan
estar to be	estando estado	está estad	estoy estás está estamos estáis están	estaré estarás estará estaremos estaréis estarán	estuve estuviste estuvo estuvimos estuvisteis estuvieron	esté estés esté estemos estéis estén
haber to have	habiendo habido	— —	he has ha hemos habéis han	habré habrás habrá habremos habréis habrán	hube hubiste hubo hubimos hubisteis hubieron	haya hayas haya hayamos hayáis hayan
hacer to do, to make	haciendo hecho	haz haced	hago haces hace hacemos hacéis hacen	haré harás hará haremos haréis harán	hice hiciste hizo hicimos hicisteis hicieron	haga hagas haga hagamos hagáis hagan

ir to go
yendo	ido	
ve	id	
voy	iré	fui
vas	irás	fuiste
va	irá	fue
vamos	iremos	fuimos
vais	iréis	fuisteis
van	irán	fueron

vaya, vayas, vaya, vayamos, vayáis, vayan

oír to hear
oyendo	oído	
oye	oíd	
oigo	oiré	oí
oyes	oirás	oíste
oye	oirá	oyó
oímos	oiremos	oímos
oís	oiréis	oísteis
oyen	oirán	oyeron

oiga, oigas, oiga, oigamos, oigáis, oigan

poder to be able
pudiendo	podido	
—	—	
puedo	podré	pude
puedes	podrás	pudiste
puede	podrá	pudo
podemos	podremos	pudimos
podéis	podréis	pudisteis
pueden	podrán	pudieron

pueda, puedas, pueda, podamos, podáis, puedan

poner to put
poniendo	puesto	
pon	poned	
pongo	pondré	puse
pones	pondrás	pusiste
pone	pondrá	puso
ponemos	pondremos	pusimos
ponéis	pondréis	pusisteis
ponen	pondrán	pusieron

ponga, pongas, ponga, pongamos, pongáis, pongan

querer to wish, to want
queriendo	querido	
quiere	quered	
quiero	querré	quise
quieres	querrás	quisiste
quiere	querrá	quiso
queremos	querremos	quisimos
queréis	querréis	quisisteis
quieren	querrán	quisieron

quiera, quieras, quiera, queramos, queráis, quieran

Verb	Participles	Commands (tú & vosotros)	Present	Future	Preterite	Present Subjunctive
saber to know	sabiendo sabido	sabe sabed	sé sabes sabe sabemos sabéis saben	sabré sabrás sabrá sabremos sabréis sabrán	supe supiste supo supimos supisteis supieron	sepa sepas sepa sepamos sepáis sepan
salir to leave	saliendo salido	sal salid	salgo sales sale salimos salís salen	saldré saldrás saldrá saldremos saldréis saldrán	salí saliste salió salimos salisteis salieron	salga salgas salga salgamos salgáis salgan
ser to be	siendo sido	sé sed	soy eres es somos sois son	seré serás será seremos seréis serán	fui fuiste fue fuimos fuisteis fueron	sea seas sea seamos seáis sean
tener to have	teniendo tenido	ten tened	tengo tienes tiene tenemos tenéis tienen	tendré tendrás tendrá tendremos tendréis tendrán	tuve tuviste tuvo tuvimos tuvisteis tuvieron	tenga tengas tenga tengamos tengáis tengan

traer — to bring

trayendo	trae	traigo	traeré	traje	traiga
traído	traed	traes	traerás	trajiste	traigas
		trae	traerá	trajo	traiga
		traemos	traeremos	trajimos	traigamos
		traéis	traeréis	trajisteis	traigáis
		traen	traerán	trajeron	traigan

valer — to be worth

valiendo	—	valgo	valdré	valí	valga
valido	—	vales	valdrás	valiste	valgas
		vale	valdrá	valió	valga
		valemos	valdremos	valimos	valgamos
		valéis	valdréis	valisteis	valgáis
		valen	valdrán	valieron	valgan

venir — to come

viniendo	ven	vengo	vendré	vine	venga
venido	venid	vienes	vendrás	viniste	vengas
		viene	vendrá	vino	venga
		venimos	vendremos	vinimos	vengamos
		venís	vendréis	vinisteis	vengáis
		vienen	vendrán	vinieron	vengan

ver — to see

viendo	ve	veo	veré	vi	vea
visto	ved	ves	verás	viste	veas
		ve	verá	vio	vea
		vemos	veremos	vimos	veamos
		veis	veréis	visteis	veáis
		ven	verán	vieron	vean

60) Revision exercises

There are ten sentences for every five chapters. Read through the appropriate chapters before doing the exercises. To help you, the chapter number is shown at the end of each sentence.

Chapters 1 to 5 Fill in the spaces with any sensible answer.

a) Quiero comprar . . . camisa, y . . . jersey. (1)
b) Va a llegar . . . por la mañana. (5)
c) Nació en . . ..(5)
d) Hay . . . alumnos en la clase. (3)
e) Deme . . . pluma. (2)
f) No tengo clase el . . .. (5)
g) Tiene muchos animales. Hay . . .. (3)
h) Ha comprado su . . . coche. (4)
i) Vas de vacaciones en . . .. (5)
j) Mamá va a hacer . . . falda y . . . vestido. (1)

Chapters 6 to 10 Fill in the spaces according to the chapter numbers. There may be several correct answers to some of the sentences.

a) Salimos del colegio a . . .. (7)
b) Los meses del . . . son diciembre, enero y febrero. (8)
c) Los chicos van . . . cine. (10)
d) La fecha de mi cumpleaños es . . .. (6)
e) Hace calor en . . .. (8)
f) Es el libro . . . niño. (10)
g) Cenamos a . . .. (7)
h) He comprado . . . pescado. (9)
i) El curso empieza en . . .. (6)
j) En la primavera . . .. (8)

Chapters 11 to 15 Fill in the spaces according to the chapter numbers. Where a verb is to be used, it is given in brackets at the end of the sentence.

a) Aquí están los discos . . . Pedro. (11)
b) (Él) . . . a su amigo. (buscar) (15a)
c) ¿Dónde . . . mis zapatos? (14)
d) ¿Por qué . . . Vd.? (trabajar) (15b)
e) Es el paraguas . . . profesor. (11)
f) . . . las once y media. (14)
g) Los alumnos . . . siempre bien. (contestar) (15a)
h) No me gusta el color . . . guantes. (11)
i) Mi hermano . . . enfermo. (14)
j) Mi madre . . . el desayuno. (preparar) (15b)

Chapters 16 to 20 Fill in the spaces according to the chapter numbers. Where a verb is to be used, it is given in brackets at the end of the sentences.

a) ¿ . . . Vd. su coche? (vender) (16a)
b) . . . voy . . . al teatro. (20)
c) Se . . . en el bar. (encontrar) (18)
d) Los niños . . . sus regalos. (abrir) (17b)
e) (Yo) . . . siempre razón. (tener) (19)
f) Mi amigo . . . tiene . . . amigos. (20)
g) Mi correspondiente no me . . . mucho. (escribir) (17a)
h) (Nosotros) . . . que acostarnos. (19)
i) (Ella) . . . un traje nuevo. (escoger) (16b)
j) ¿A qué hora . . . tu padre? (volver) (18)

Chapters 21 to 25 Fill in the spaces according to the chapter numbers. Where a verb is to be used, it is given in brackets at the end of the sentence.

a) ¿ . . . no estás escuchando? (25)
b) . . . Vd. el vino, por favor. (pasar) (23)
c) La chica . . .. (peinarse) (22b)
d) Veré . . . María mañana. (24)
e) (Yo) . . . antes de desayunar. (vestirse) (22a)
f) No . . . (tú) la ventana. (cerrar) (23)
g) ¿ . . . viven tus abuelos? (25)
h) Vamos a encontrar . . . nuestros amigos. (24)
i) El sol . . . (ponerse) (22b)
j) Niño, . . . aquí. (venir) (23)

Chapters 26 to 30 Fill in the spaces according to the chapter numbers. Adjectives to be used are given in brackets at the end of the sentence.

a) Mercedes tiene una falda . . .. (nuevo) (28)
b) ¿Vives . . . España? (26)
c) Va a llegar . . . moto. (27)
d) ¿Dónde están . . . guantes? (your – *fam. plur.*) (30)
e) Ha venido en . . . coche. (her) (30)
f) Papá lleva zapatos . . .. (marrón) (28)
g) No hay . . . ruido. (ninguno) (29)
h) Viene . . . Londres. (26)
i) Mi madre es una . . . mujer. (grande) (29)
j) Le gusta dar un paseo . . . caballo. (27)

Chapters 31 to 35 Fill in the spaces according to the chapter numbers.

a) Aquí está la foto. ¿Es . . . ? (his) No, es . . .. (hers) (31)
b) Ha comido . . . las fresas. (34)
c) Es la casa . . . de la ciudad. (grande) (35)

d) Este vestido es de Isabel; . . . es de Teresa. (33)
e) Me gustan . . . manzanas. (32)
f) ¿Has hecho tus deberes? He hecho . . .. (mine) (31)
g) Lo he bebido . . .. (34)
h) Deme . . . libro. (that) (32)
i) Pablo es . . . perezoso . . . su hermano. (35)
j) ¿Qué es . . .? (that) (33)

Chapters 36 to 40 Change the words in **bold print** into object pronouns, future tense, etc., or fill in the blanks according to the chapter numbers.

a) Nosotros nadamos bien, pero tú nadas . . .. (36)
b) Da **la pluma a su amigo.** (39)
c) ¡Mande **las cartas al director!** (40)
d) El coche anda . . .. (36)
e) **Llegamos** a las seis. (37, 38)
f) Quiero prestar **los lápices a mi hermana.** (39)
g) **Hay** mucha gente en el teatro. (37)
h) No muestres **tus deberes a Juan.** (40)
i) No **salgo** antes de las ocho. (37, 38)
j) **Nos paseamos** en el campo. (37, 38)

Chapters 41 to 45 Fill in the spaces according to the chapter numbers. Any verbs to be used are given in brackets at the end of the sentence.

a) No me acuerdo de . . .. (him) (41)
b) (Nosotros) . . . al cine ayer. (ir) (43)
c) ¿Dónde . . . Vd. el periódico? (poner) (44)
d) ¿Has terminado tus deberes? Sí, . . . terminarlos. (45)
e) (Ellos) . . . en Barcelona desde hace un año. (vivir) (45)
f) ¿Vas a venir con . . .? (me) (41)
g) (Yo) . . . en Londres esta semana. (estar) (44)
h) (Ella) . . . temprano esta mañana. (levantarse) (42)
i) (Ellos) . . . que no iban a venir. (decir) (43)
j) Vd. . . . al autobús delante de mí. (subir) (42)

Chapters 46 to 50 Fill in the spaces according to the chapter numbers. Any verbs to used are given in brackets at the end of the sentence.

a) (Él) . . . bien cuando era joven. (nadar) (46)
b) Dije que . . . a París. (ir) (48)
c) Aquí está el chico con . . . sale. (49)
d) Aquí está la dirección de la oficina a . . . tienes que escribir. (50)
e) (Ellas) . . . todos los días al mercado. (ir) (46)
f) La clase . . ., cuando llegó. (empezar) (47)
g) Ha encontrado los juguetes con . . . el niño jugaba. (50)

h) ¿Ha visto Vd. al hombre . . . vende helados? (49)
i) Me . . . comprar una casa. (gustar) (48)
j) Ya . . . cuando llamaste. (salir) (47)

Chapters 51 to 55 Fill in the spaces according to the chapter numbers. Any verbs to be used are given in brackets at the end of the sentence.

a) Estaré triste cuando (tú) . . .. (salir) (51)
b) Las niñas . . . a las siete. (acostarse) (55)
c) ¡ . . . por favor! (53)
d) . . . turrón por Navidad en España. (comer) (54)
e) Si . . . tiempo, iré a verte. (tener) (52)
f) Aquí . . . español. (hablar) (54)
g) Deseamos que (vosotros) lo . . . bien. (pasar) (51)
h) La abuela . . . en su sillón. (53)
i) Por fin, (él) . . . hacerlo. (conseguir) (55)
j) Si (tú) . . . bueno, te compraré un regalo. (ser) (52)

Index

Numbers given refer to *chapter numbers*. Spanish words are printed in **bold type**. Some terms may be explained further at the front of the book. (See *Explanation of English terms used*.)